ADDISON WESLEY

Math Makes Sense 2

Author Team

Carole Saundry
Heather Spencer
Maureen Dockendorf
Maggie Martin Connell
Linden Gray
Sharon Jeroski
Michelle Jackson
Sandra Ball
Jill Norman
Susan Green

PEARSON
Addison Wesley

Elementary Math Team Leader
Anne-Marie Scullion

Publisher
Claire Burnett

Publishing Team
Enid Haley
Lesley Haynes
Tricia Carmichael
Lynn Pereira
Rosalyn Steiner
Ellen Davidson
Sarah Mawson
Eileen Pyne-Rudzik
Stephanie Cox
Kaari Turk
Judy Wilson
Nicole Argyropoulos

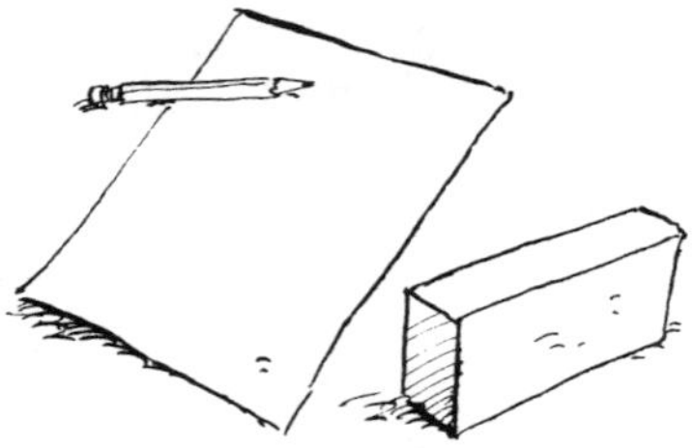

Product Manager
Nishaant Sanghavi

Photo Research
Karen Hunter

Design
Word & Image Design Studio Inc.

ISBN 0-321-24222-X

Printed and bound in Canada
5 6 7 CP 15 14 13

Acknowledgments
The publisher wishes to thank the following sources for photographs, illustrations, and other materials used in this text. Care has been taken to determine and locate ownership of copyright material in this book. We will gladly receive information enabling us to rectify any errors or omissions in credits.

Cover
Cover illustration by Marisol Sarrazin

Illustrations
June Bradford, pp. 87–90, 189–192, 281–284
Kasia Charko, p. 253
Virginie Faucher, pp. 141, 214–234
Marie-Claude Favreau, pp. 1–12, 75–86, 177–188, 269–280
Eugenie Fernandes, p. 193
Joanne Fitzgerald, pp. 88–90, 236–252
Leanne Franson, p. 153
Linda Hendry, pp. 115–132
Tina Holdcroft, pp. 53–61, 63, 66–71, 73, 74, 154–176
Vesna Krstanovic, pp. 27–29, 31–49, 52, 194–212, 217
André Labrie, pp. 13–26
Bernadette Lau, pp. 50, 51, 110
Paul McCusker, pp. 64, 65, 104, 107, 151
Marc Mongeau, pp. 213, 235
Allan Moon, pp. 11, 30, 43, 44, 61–63, 72, 74, 118, 119, 121, 122, 135, 137–140, 144–149, 208, 209
Scott Ritchie, pp. 91–94, 96–103, 105–109, 111–114, 190–192, 254–268, 281–284
Bill Slavin, pp. 133–152
Pat Stephens, p. 95
Neil Stewart, Math at Home tech art

PEARSON
Addison Wesley

Contents

Program Consultants and Advisers

Program Consultants

Craig Featherstone
Maggie Martin Connell
Trevor Brown

Assessment Consultant
Sharon Jeroski

Primary Mathematics and Literacy Consultant
Pat Dickinson

Elementary Mathematics Adviser
John A. Van de Walle

British Columbia Early Numeracy Adviser
Carole Saundry

Ontario Early Math Strategy Adviser
Ruth Dawson

Program Advisers

Pearson Education thanks its Program Advisers, who helped shape the vision for *Addison Wesley Mathematics Makes Sense* through discussions and reviews of prototype materials and manuscript.

Anthony Azzopardi
Bob Belcher
Judy Blake
Steve Cairns
Daryl Chichak
Lynda Colgan
Marg Craig
Jennifer Gardner
Florence Glanfield
Pamela Hagen
Dennis Hamaguchi
Angie Harding
Peggy Hill
Auriana Kowalchuk
Gordon Li
Werner Liedtke
Jodi Mackie
Kristi Manuel
Lois Marchand
Cathy Molinski
Bill Nimigon
Eileen Phillips
Evelyn Sawicki
Shannon Sharp
Lynn Strangway
Mignonne Wood

Program Reviewers

Field Testers

Pearson Education thanks the teachers and students who field-tested *Addison Wesley Math Makes Sense 2* prior to publication. Their feedback and constructive recommendations have been most valuable in helping us to develop a quality mathematics program.

Aboriginal Content Reviewers

Early Childhood and School Services Division, Department of Education, Culture, and Employment, Government of Northwest Territories:

Steven Daniel, Coordinator, Mathematics, Science, and Secondary Education
Liz Fowler, Coordinator, Culture-Based Education
Margaret Erasmus, Coordinator, Aboriginal Languages

Grade 2 Reviewers

Anne Boyd
School District 72 (Campbell River), BC

Bob Belcher
Sooke School District, BC

Judy Blake
School District 44 (North Vancouver), BC

Trevor Brown
Course Director, Mathematics Education, OISE/UT, ON

Ralph Connelly
Coordinator, Halton District School Board, ON

Marg Craig
Independent Mathematics Consultant, ON

Ruth Dawson
Coordinator, Halton District School Board, ON

Lorelei Gibeau
Edmonton Catholic Separate School District, AB

Werner Liedtke
University of Victoria, BC

Lois Marchand
Independent Consultant, AB

Livia Paradis
Edmonton Catholic School Board, AB

Gillian Parsons
Elementary Program Co-ordinator, Brant Haldimand-Norfolk Catholic School Board, ON

Lynn Strangway
Toronto District School Board, ON

Roz Thomson
Halton District School Board, ON

School Begins

"It's time for school," Cam's grandma said.
"Open your eyes. Get out of bed.
I'm coming to school today with you,
because you're starting somewhere new."

Take-Home Story

"I'm scared," Cam said, then chewed his toast.
He hated changing schools the most.
"I won't have friends."
Then Grandma sighed.
"You'll make *new* friends, Cam," she replied.

The teacher greeted them at the door,
and welcomed Cam to Classroom 4.
The chairs and tables were tightly fit.
Cam looked around. "Where should I sit?"

The teacher pointed. "There's a chair.
You can sit with those children there.
Your grandma can sit at that table, too,
if she'd like to stay awhile with you."

The teacher asked Grandma, “Can you help today?
We’re learning math games we can play.
There are materials to share and rules to learn,
like when to move and take a turn.”

Cam's group listened to the teacher explain.
She repeated some of the rules again.
She said, “Do you have questions? Raise your hand.”
But the class said, “No, we understand.”

At recess, Grandma had to go.
She said, "This is the best Grade 2 I know!"
She waved at all her new young friends,
who called, "Come back, and help again!"

About the Story

The story was read in class to prepare for a Mathematics Investigation activity. Children played a variety of mathematical games and created addition and subtraction stories. The Investigation provided opportunities for the teacher to learn about children's mathematical understanding and skills as they begin a new school year.

Talk about It Together

- How did Cam feel about his first day of school?
- What do you think Cam's math class will be like? Why?
- What did Cam's teacher do to help the children work together?
- How is Cam's classroom the same as your classroom? How is it different?

At the Library

Ask your local librarian about books with math-related themes that are appropriate for Grade 2 readers.

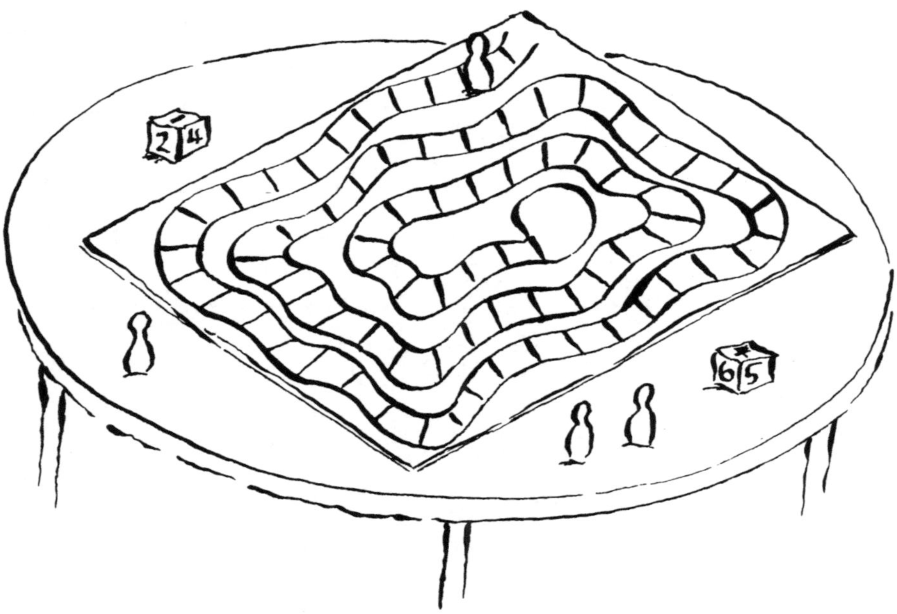

Grandma Helps

Make a number story about the picture.
Use pictures, numbers, or words to tell your story.

Race to 100!

Roll 2 number cubes.
Add the numbers.
Take that number of Snap Cubes.

Every time you have 10 Snap Cubes,
put them together to make a 10-stick.
Stop when you have 10 sticks. They will total 100 cubes!

Estimate. How many rolls will you need to get 100 cubes?
Show your thinking in pictures, numbers, or words.

Keep track. Make a ✓ for each roll.
When you reach 100, count your ✓.

How many rolls altogether? _______

Building Challenge!

Use a spinner.
Try to build the tallest structure you can.
You can spin 10 times. Which spinner will you choose?

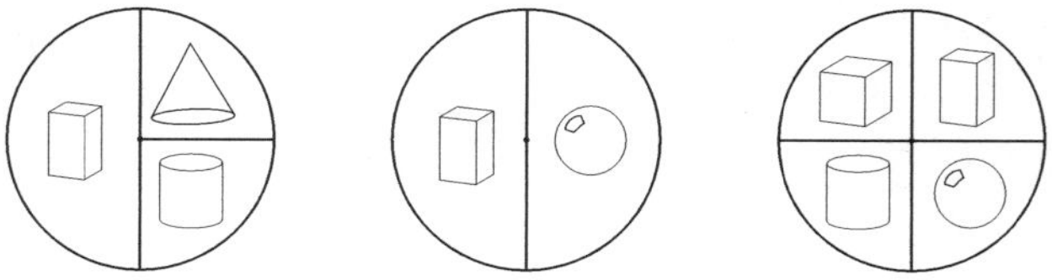

Show your thinking in pictures, numbers, or words.

Spin 10 times.
Each time you spin, take the object you landed on.
Tell how many of each you have.

3-D Object	How Many I Have	How Many I Used
cone		
cylinder		
sphere		
cube		
prism		

Use your 10-stick to measure your structure.

How tall is it? ________ 10-sticks

A Special Game

Make your own math game.
You can use spinners, number cubes, counters, solids, or anything you like.

Tell how to play your game.

What do you need to play your game?

Write the rules to your game.

Teach other children how to play your game.

UNIT 1

Sorting and Patterning

Focus | Children discuss how the tools and supplies are sorted in the picture.

Name: ______________________ Date: ______________________

Dear Family,

Your child is starting a unit in mathematics on sorting and patterning.

The Learning Goals for this unit are to

- Sort objects according to attributes, such as colour, size, and shape.
- Describe, extend, and draw patterns.
- Talk about a pattern rule.
- Use two attributes to make a pattern.

You can help your child achieve these goals by doing the Home Connection activities suggested at the bottom of selected pages.

Name: ______________________ Date: ______________________

Clean-Up Time

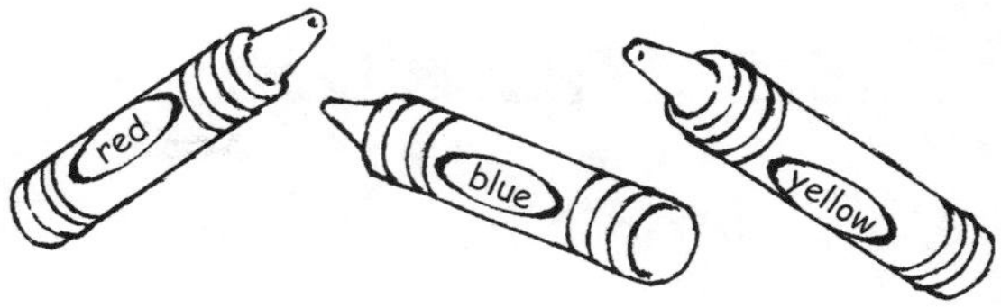

Help the carpenter clean up her bench.

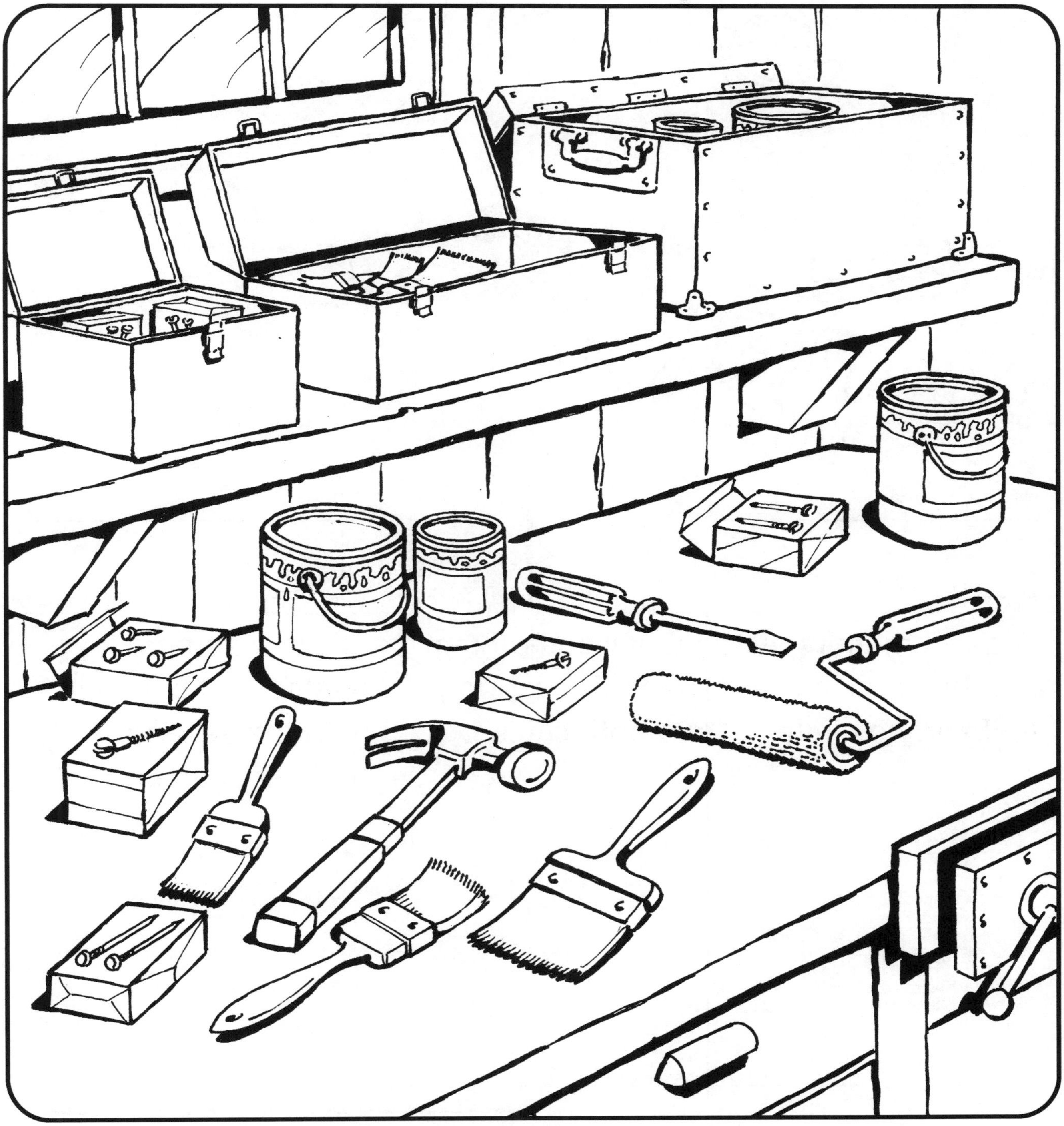

Focus | Children sort items into bins by colouring each bin a different colour and then, colouring each item to match the bin where that item belongs. There are multiple correct answers.

Name: ______________________ Date: ______________________

Find the Rule

Write labels in the boxes to tell how the clothing is sorted.

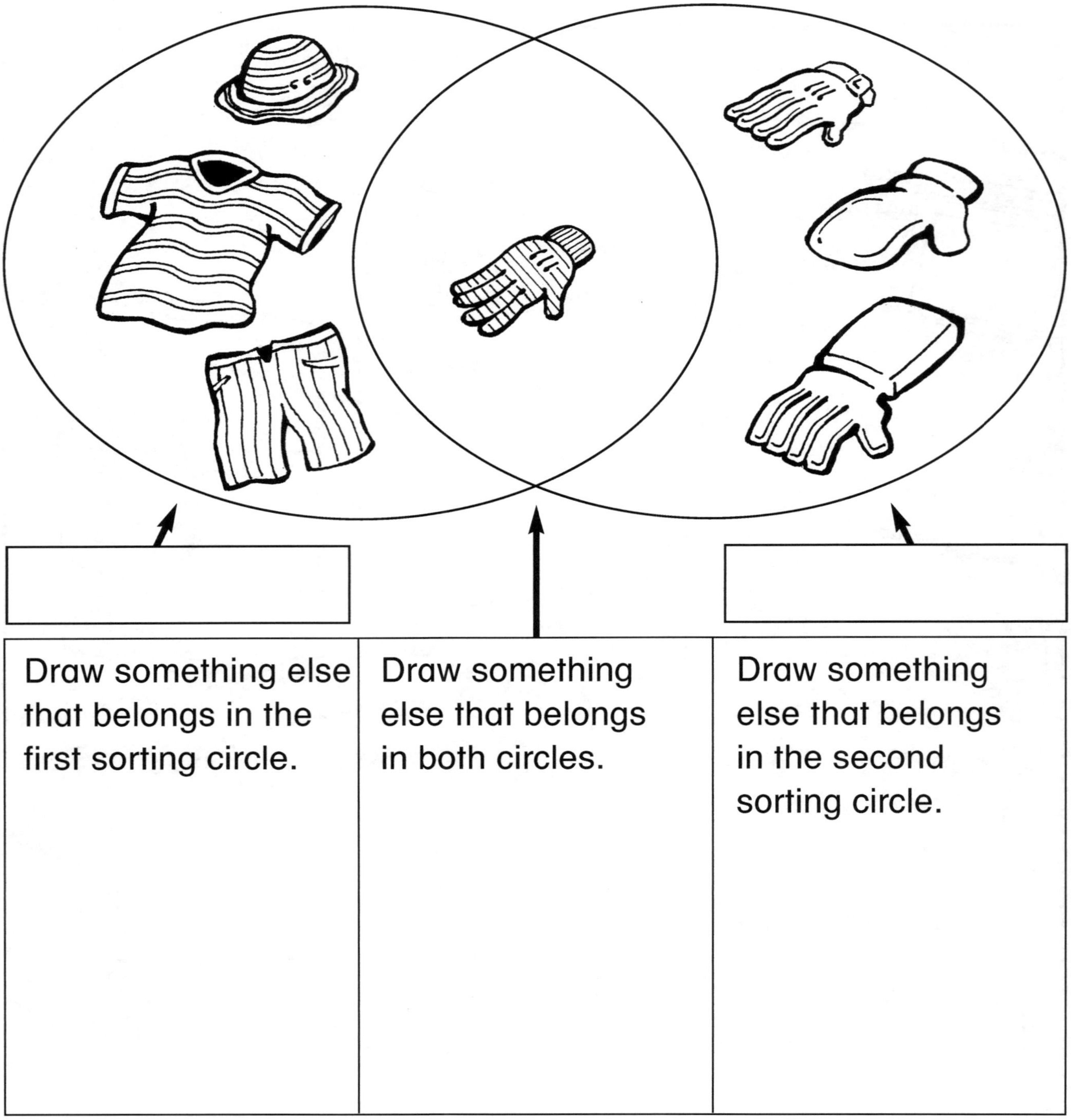

Draw something else that belongs in the first sorting circle.	Draw something else that belongs in both circles.	Draw something else that belongs in the second sorting circle.

Focus | Children identify the sorting rule and label the sorting circles. They draw other items that belong in each group.

HOME CONNECTION

Ask your child: "Why do we sort laundry before washing it and putting it away? What other things do we sort?"

Name: ______________________ Date: ______________________

Make Your Own Patterns

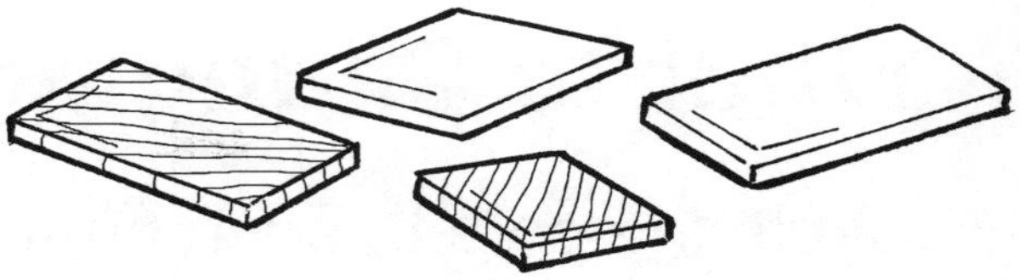

Use Attribute Blocks.

Make a pattern with 2 changing attributes. Draw it here.

Circle the pattern core.

List the changing attributes. ______________ ______________

Use the same 2 attributes.

Make a different pattern. Draw it here.

Circle the pattern core.

How are the patterns the same?

____

How are they different?

____

Focus | Children make and record patterns with two changing attributes.

Name: ______________________ Date: ______________________

What Is Changing?

Circle the core in each pattern.
What 2 attributes are changing in each pattern?

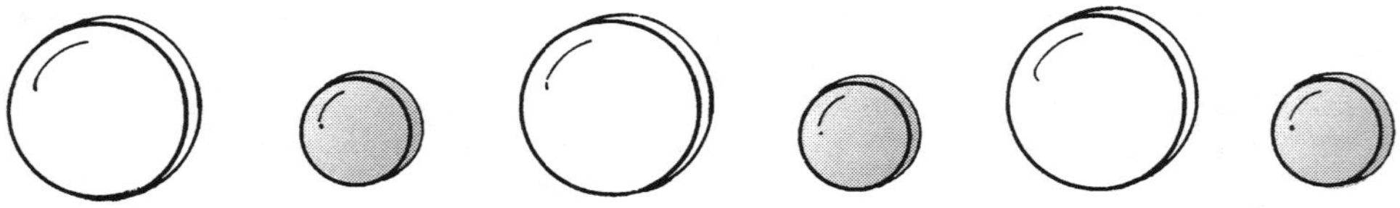

______________________ ______________________

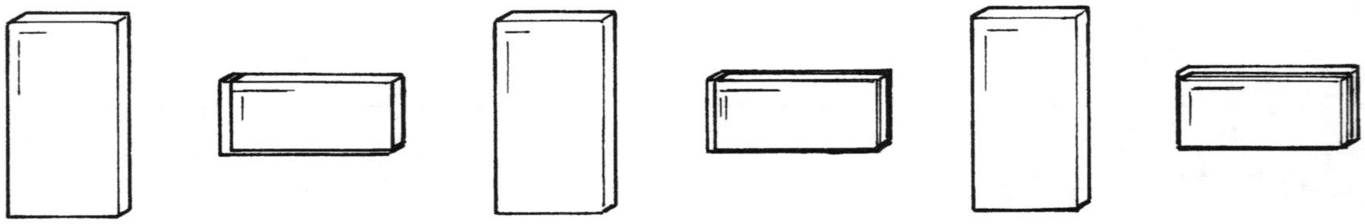

______________________ ______________________

______________________ ______________________

Make a pattern. Draw it here.

Focus | Children identify two changing attributes in various patterns. Then, they make their own pattern.

Name: ______________________________ Date: ______________________________

Making Patterns

Make a pattern. Use 6 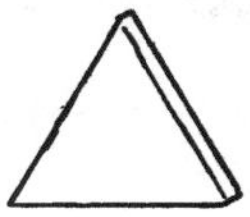 and 9 .

Look at a friend's pattern. How are the patterns the same?

____

How are the patterns different?

____

How did you know how to arrange the objects?

____

____

Focus | Children make and compare patterns with two changing attributes. There are multiple correct answers.

HOME CONNECTION

Have your child use large red and small green circles to make a pattern in two different ways. Ask: "How are the patterns the same? How are they different?"

Name: ______________________ Date: ______________________

Make the Same Pattern

Look at the Snap Cube pattern.

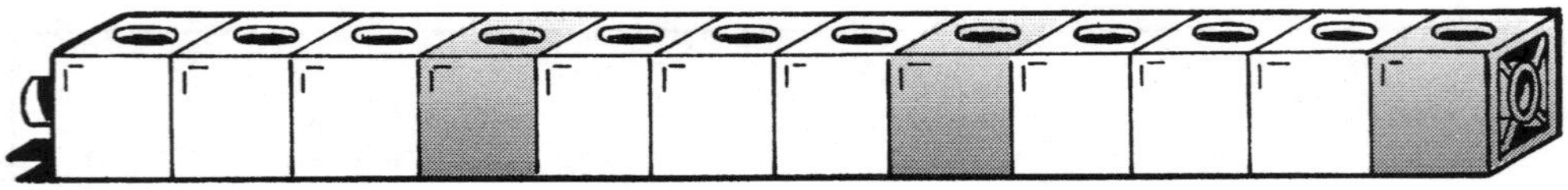

Here is another way to show the pattern.

Draw two other ways to show the pattern.

Focus | Children represent the same pattern in different ways.

Name: ______________________ Date: ______________________

Picture Patterns

Draw pictures to show the patterns.

tall, short; tall, short; tall, short

red, blue, green; red, blue, green; red, blue, green

Use words to write your own pattern.

____

____

Ask a friend to draw your pattern.

Focus | Children use picture patterns to represent word patterns.

HOME CONNECTION

Look around your home with your child for patterns. Ask your child to draw a picture to represent each pattern.

Name: ______________________ Date: ______________________

Name That Pattern

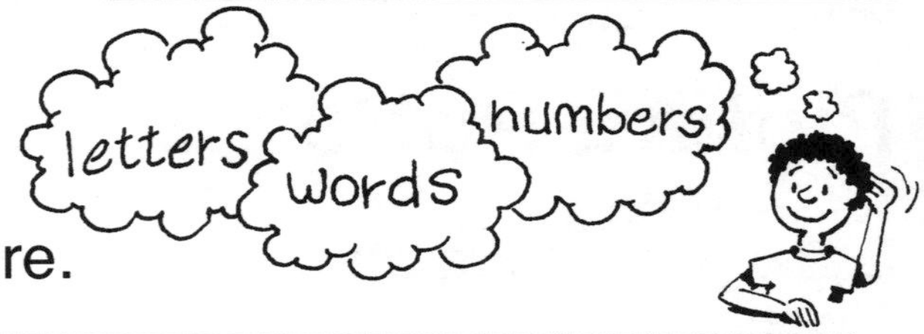

Use words to describe the pattern core.

____

Use letters to record the pattern.

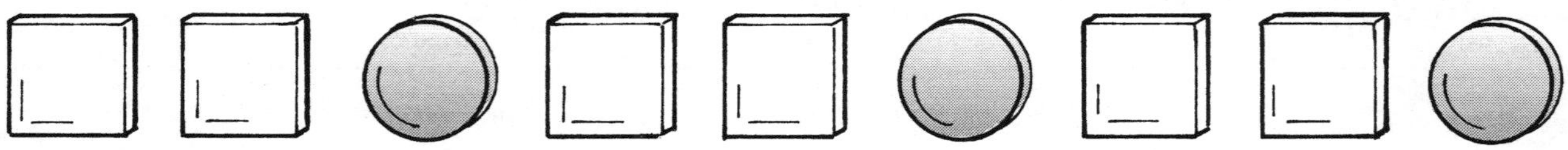

___ ___ ___ ___ ___ ___ ___ ___ ___

Use numbers to record the pattern.

___ ___ ___ ___ ___ ___ ___ ___ ___ ___ ___ ___

Draw a pattern. Ask a friend to record the pattern in another way.

____

Focus I Children represent patterns in different ways. There are multiple correct answers.

Name: ______________________ Date: ______________________

Use All the Beads

There are 9 red, 3 green, and 6 blue beads.

Make a pattern.
Use all the beads.

Show your thinking in pictures, numbers, or words.

Focus | Children use all the beads to make a pattern. There are multiple correct answers.

Name: ______________________________ Date: ______________________________

Bead Pattern

There are 3 blue, 6 red, and 6 green beads.

Make a pattern.
Use all the beads.

Show your thinking in pictures, numbers, or words.

Focus | Children use all the beads to make a pattern. There are multiple correct answers.

HOME CONNECTION

Ask your child: "Can you make a different pattern using all the beads? Show me."

Name: ______________________ Date: ______________________

My Pattern Border

Draw the pattern for your placemat and describe it.

____

____

HOME CONNECTION

With your child, make a pattern using crayons, markers, stickers, pencils, or other favourite objects. Change the order of objects and make another pattern.

Focus | Children draw and describe the patterns they will use.

Name: ______________________ Date: ______________________

My Journal

Tell what you learned about using 2 attributes to sort.

Tell what you learned about using 2 changing attributes to make a pattern.

Focus | Children reflect on what they have learned about sorting and patterning.

UNIT 2

Number Relationships

Focus | Children talk about the picture and identify numbers of objects.

Name: ______________________ Date: ______________________

Dear Family,

This unit will focus on deepening your child's understanding of number relationships, counting, and place value.

The Learning Goals for this unit are to

- Read and print number words to 20.
- Build numbers with concrete materials.
- Estimate the number of objects and check by counting.
- Count forward to 100 and backward from 20 using a number line, a 100-chart, and a calculator.
- Count by 1s, 2s, 5s, 10s, and 25s.
- Develop strategies for adding and subtracting.

You can help your child achieve these goals by doing the Home Connection activities suggested at the bottom of selected pages.

Name: ______________________ Date: ______________________

How Many?

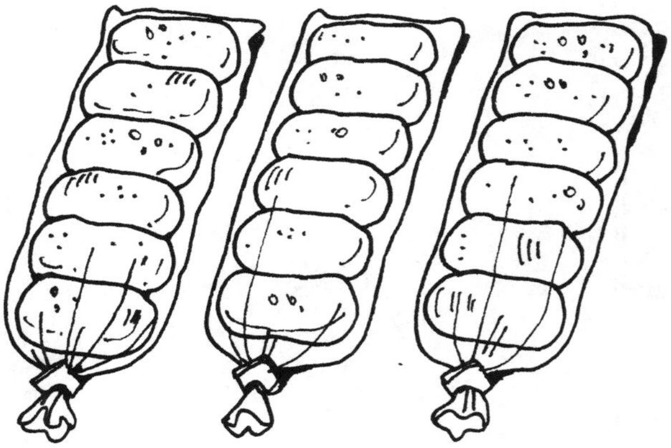

How many rolls? ________

How many eggs? ________

How many buns? ________

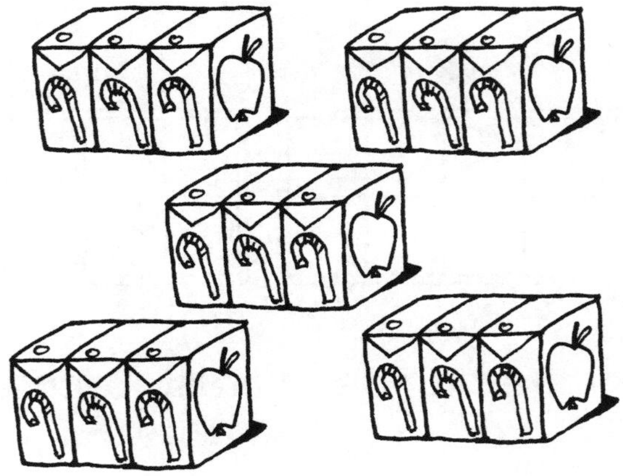

How many boxes? ________

What groups of items show the same number?

____

How do you know?

____

Focus | Children count and record the number in each group and determine what groups show the same number.

Name: ________________________ Date: ________________________

Numbers to 20

Draw counters to show how many. Record the numerals.

twelve

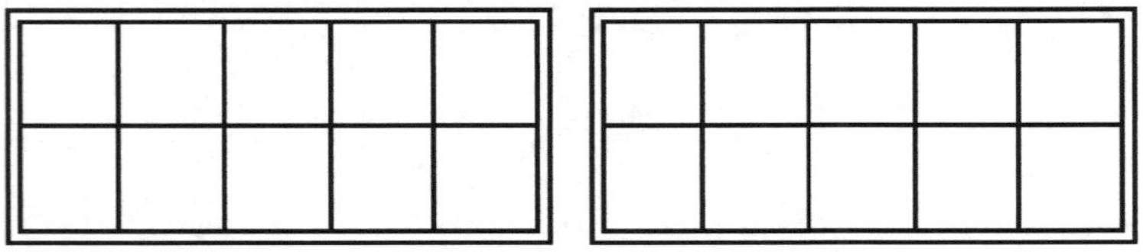

________ is 10 and ________.

nineteen

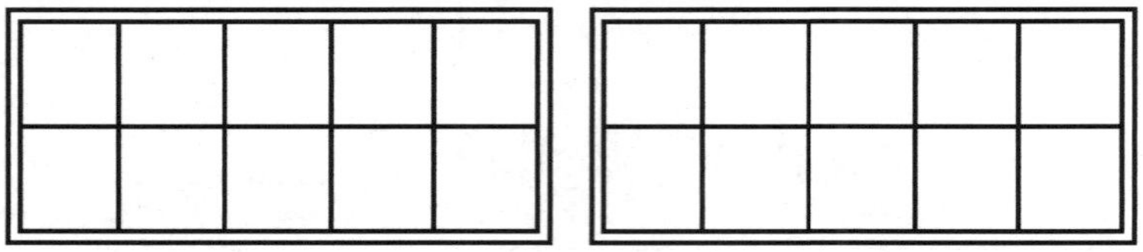

________ is 10 and ________.

fourteen

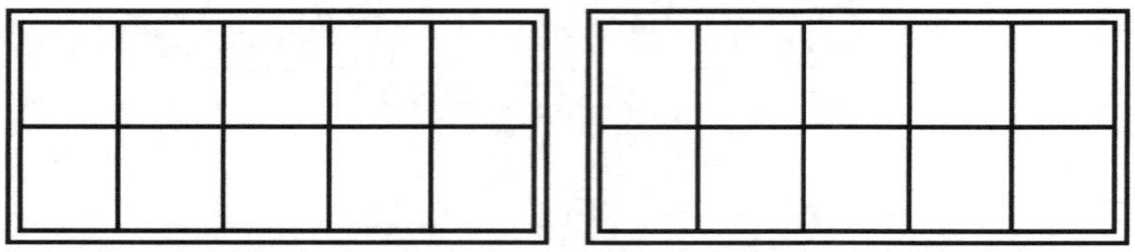

________ is 10 and ________.

Print the number words. Record the numerals.

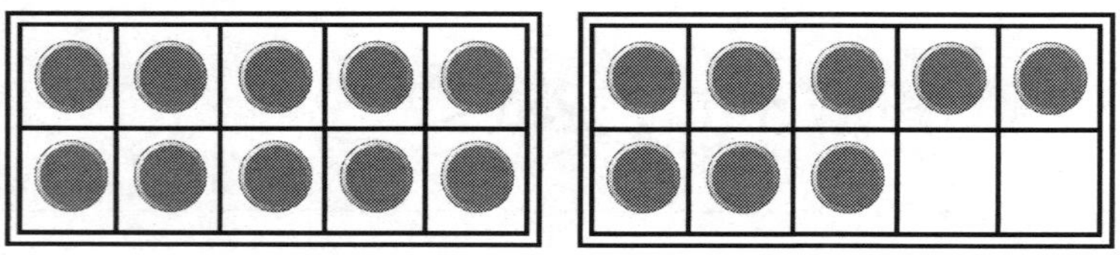

____

________ is 10 and ________.

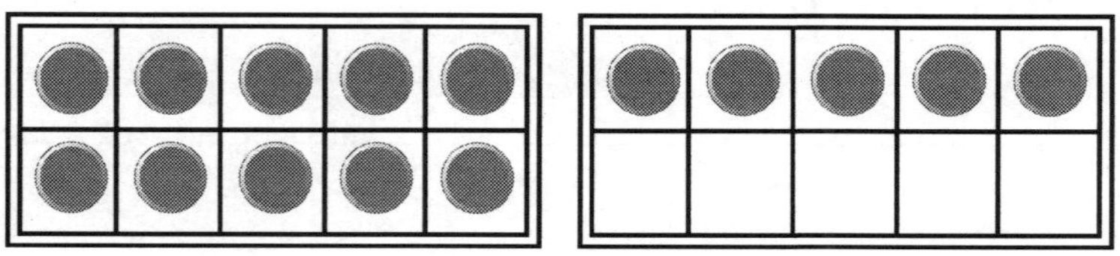

____

________ is 10 and ________.

Focus | Children use ten-frames to record and identify numbers to 20.

HOME CONNECTION

Have your child explain how to use a ten-frame. Ask: "How would you use a ten-frame to show 11? To show 17?"

Name: ____________________ Date: ____________________

Counting Two Ways

Spill the objects. Estimate the number. _______
You will count all the objects.

As you begin counting, look back at your estimate.
If you want, make a new estimate. _______

Tell how you counted. Use pictures, numbers, or words.

Spill the objects again. Count them another way.
Tell how you counted. Use pictures, numbers, or words.

Focus | Children estimate the number in a collection of up to 50 objects and then count the objects in 2 different ways. They describe how they counted using pictures, numbers, or words.

Name: ______________________ Date: ______________________

Count the Buttons

How many buttons are there? _______

Tell how you counted. Use pictures, numbers, or words.

What other way could you count the buttons?

____

____

HOME CONNECTION

Gather a collection of about 40 small objects for your child to count, such as raisins or pennies. Ask your child to count the collection by grouping the objects in different ways.

Focus | Children count a collection using a strategy of their choice.

Name: ______________________________ Date: ______________________________

What Is Missing?

Write the missing numerals on the number lines.

8 ☐ 10 ☐ 12 13 14 ☐ ☐ 17 18

☐ 27 28 ☐ 30 31 ☐ 33 ☐ ☐ 36

39 ☐ ☐ 42 43 44 ☐ ☐ ☐ 48 ☐

Write numerals on the number line for these number words:
fifteen, eighteen, twenty, twenty-two.

☐ 16 ☐ ☐ 19 ☐ ☐ ☐ 23 24 ☐

What numerals are still missing? ______________________________
Write these numerals on the number line.

HOME CONNECTION
Help your child find some examples where number lines are used, such as on a thermometer or on a map showing the map scale.

Focus | Children complete partial number lines by writing missing numerals.

Name: ______________________ Date: ______________________

Number Sentences

Write each number sentence.

___ + ___ = ___

___ + ___ = ___

___ − ___ = ___

___ − ___ = ___

Make your own

___ ◯ ___ = ___

Focus | Children write number sentences about the pictures. They draw a picture to represent a number sentence.

Name: ______________________ Date: ______________________

Garden Problems

Write each number sentence.

There are 9  in a garden.

4 are yellow. The rest are pink.

How many  are pink?

_____ ◯ _____ = _____

There were 13  on a tree.
Some fell off.

Now there are 6  on the tree.

How many fell off?

_____ ◯ _____ = _____

There are 15  in the yard.

8  are in a tree.

The rest are on a fence.
How many are on the fence?

_____ ◯ _____ = _____

A  puts 7  in a pile.

The squirrel gathers some more.

Now there are 16 .

How many more did the  gather?

_____ ◯ _____ = _____

Focus | Children write number sentences to represent addition- and subtraction-story problems.

HOME CONNECTION

Share addition and subtraction story problems about things in your neighbourhood. For example, "There are 15 houses on our street. 9 of them have a garage. How many do not have a garage?"

Name: ______________________ Date: ______________________

Snappy Number Sentences

Use Snap Cubes. 

Complete the number sentences.

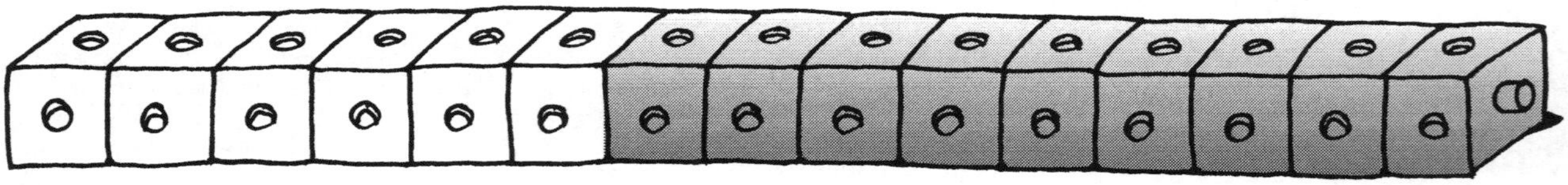

_____ + _____ = _____ _____ − _____ = _____

_____ + _____ = _____ _____ − _____ = _____

_____ + _____ = _____ _____ − _____ = _____

_____ + _____ = _____ _____ − _____ = _____

_____ + _____ = _____ _____ − _____ = _____

_____ + _____ = _____ _____ − _____ = _____

How does knowing 7 + 6 help when finding 13 − 6?

____

Focus | Children write addition and subtraction sentences to describe arrangements of Snap Cubes. They explain how knowing an addition fact helps find the answer to a subtraction fact.

Name: ______________________ Date: ______________________

Add or Subtract

$$\begin{array}{r}15\\+3\\\hline\end{array}\qquad\begin{array}{r}9\\+7\\\hline\end{array}\qquad\begin{array}{r}11\\-2\\\hline\end{array}\qquad\begin{array}{r}14\\-6\\\hline\end{array}$$

13 + 2 = _____ 13 − 5 = _____ 17 − 1 = _____ 15 − 8 = _____

Choose a question. Tell about the strategy you used to solve it.
Use pictures, numbers, or words.

Find the missing numbers. Use counters to model your answer.

15 − ☐ = 6 17 − ☐ = 8 13 − ☐ = 6 15 − ☐ = 7

FOCUS | Children use strategies to complete addition and subtraction sentences.

HOME CONNECTION

Have your child build a set of 11 to 15 pennies and then add 1, 2, or 3 to that number. Have your child count on from that number to get the total. Repeat the activity for subtraction.

Name: ______________________________ Date: ______________________________

Seeing Doubles

Finish each picture to show a double.
Write the addition sentence.

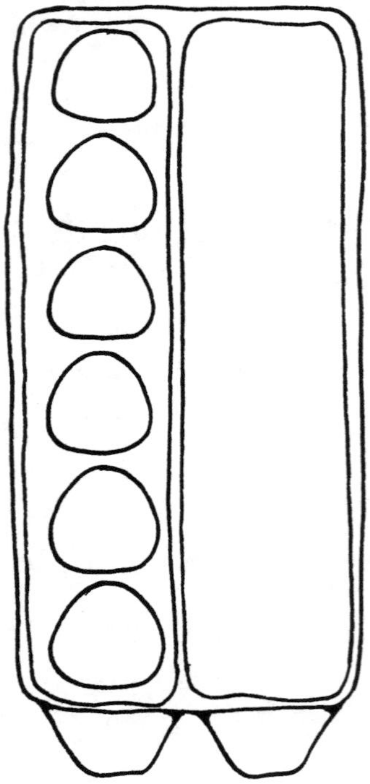	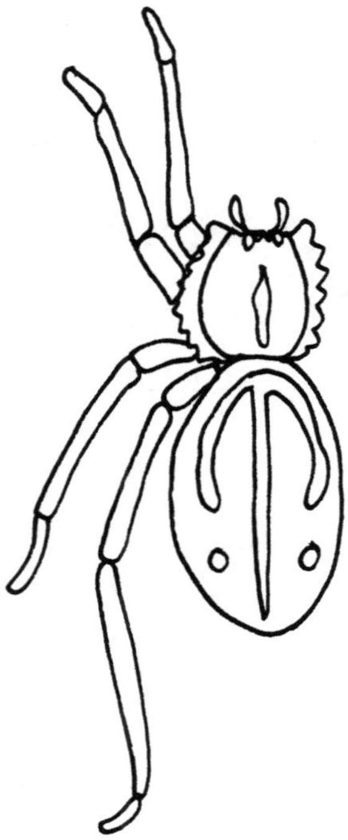	
____ + ____ = ____	____ + ____ = ____	____ + ____ = ____

Circle the numeral that is not the answer for a doubles addition story.

4	8	9	10	16

How do you know?

____

____

____

Focus | Children draw to show doubles and record the doubles facts.

Name: ______________________ Date: ______________________

Using Doubles

Write 2 doubles facts that can help you find the answers.

6 + 7 = ____ ____ + ____ = ____ ____ + ____ = ____	4 + 5 = ____ ____ + ____ = ____ ____ + ____ = ____	3 + 2 = ____ ____ + ____ = ____ ____ + ____ = ____
7 + 8 = ____ ____ + ____ = ____ ____ + ____ = ____	4 + 3 = ____ ____ + ____ = ____ ____ + ____ = ____	9 + 8 = ____ ____ + ____ = ____ ____ + ____ = ____

HOME CONNECTION
Ask your child to tell a number story using a double or near doubles.

Focus | Children use doubles facts to find answers to near doubles.

Name: ______________________ Date: ______________________

About How Many?

Spill the counters.
Make one group of 10.

Estimate the total number. It is about _____.

Make groups of 10s to show how you counted.
Use pictures, numbers, or words.

_______ groups of 10s and _______ left over _______ in all

HOME CONNECTION

Gather about 60 small objects (pennies, paper clips). Ask: "About how many objects are there?" Have your child make groups of 10s, count the number of 10s, and count on to find the total.

Focus | Children use a group of 10 to estimate a total, then count groups of 10s and leftover 1s to determine the total.

Name: ______________________ Date: ______________________

Full of Beans

Take a handful of beans with both hands.
Estimate the number.
Think of grouping by 10s.

Circle your estimate.
- more than 50
- fewer than 50

Make one group of 10.
Change your estimate if you wish. _____

Place the beans in the ten-frames.
Colour to show your work.

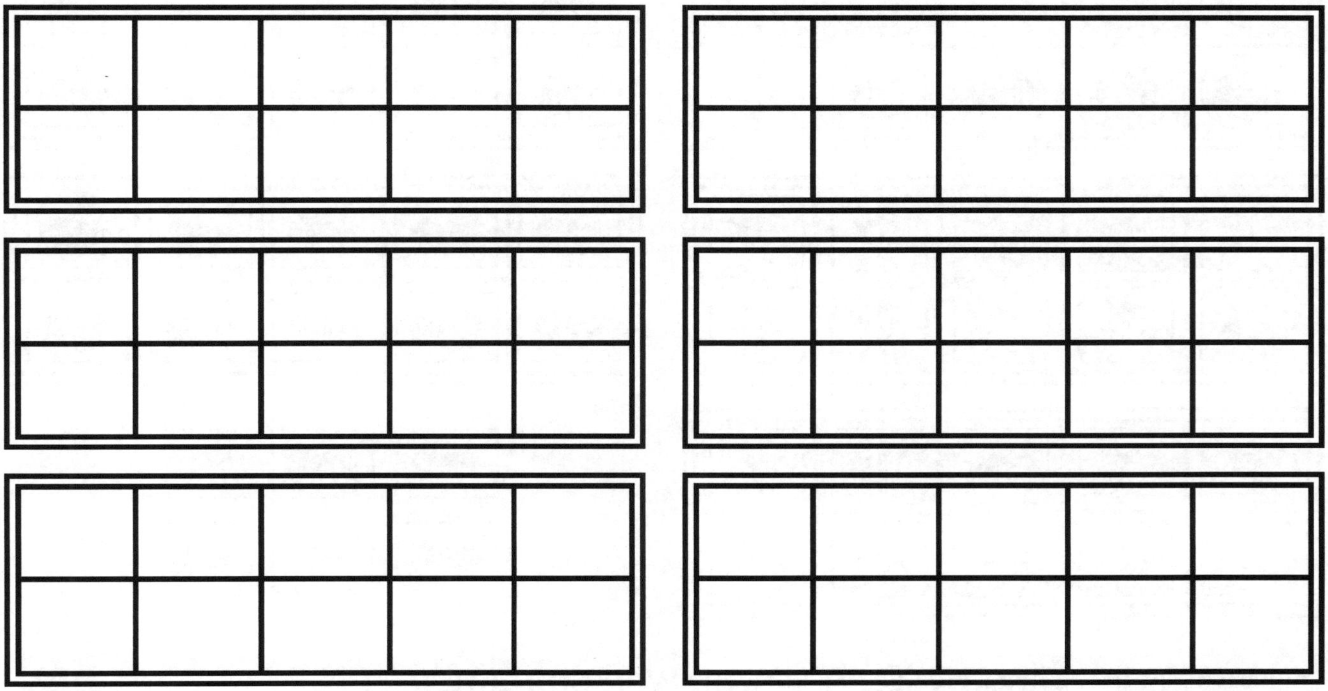

________ groups of 10s and ________ left over ________ in all

Focus | Children take a handful of beans and estimate the number. Then, they place the beans on the ten-frames and count to check their estimates. They colour the ten-frames to record their work.

Name: ______________________________ Date: ______________________________

Counting by 10s

Circle groups of 10 ants.
Record the numbers.

________ groups of 10s and ________ left over ________ in all

Rouda used ten-frames to organize her sticker collection.
How many stickers does she have?

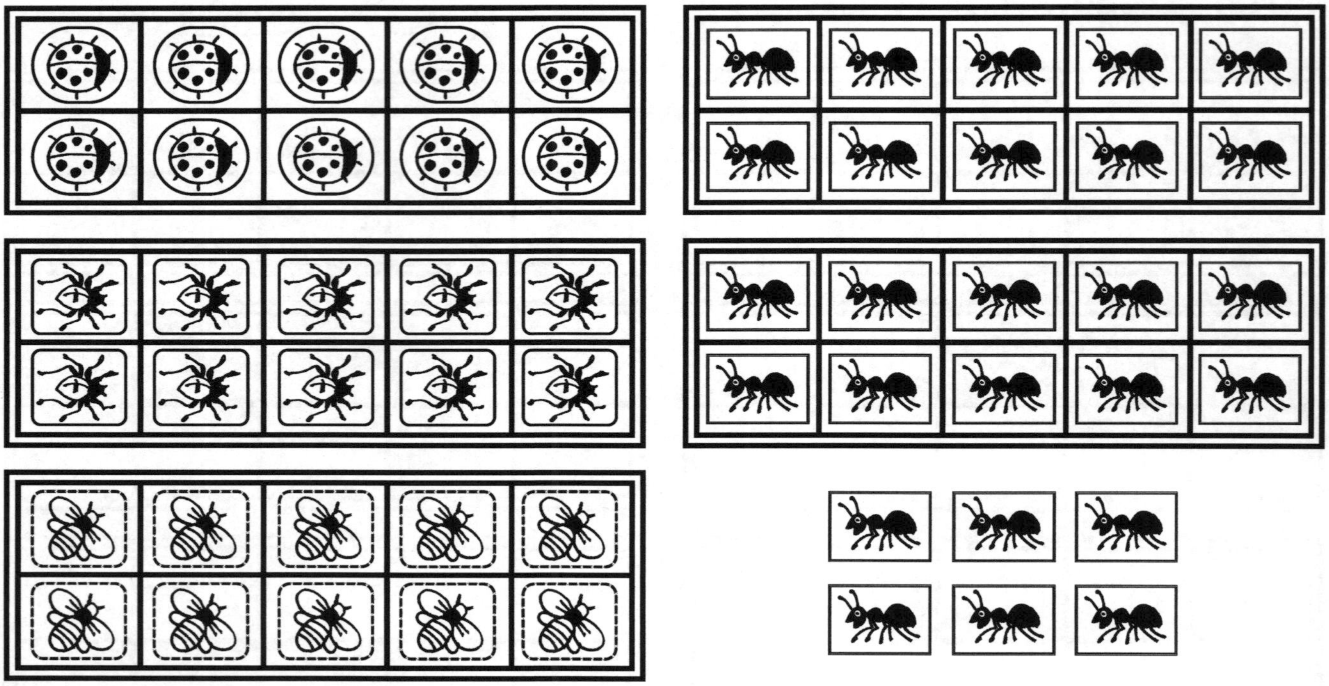

How can grouping by 10s help you with counting?

____

____

Focus | Children make groups of 10s and record the number of 10s, the leftover ones, and the total.

Name: ______________________________ Date: ______________________________

Be a Number Detective

Each piece of a 100-chart is missing some numerals.
Look for clues in the numbers to help you fill in the empty spaces.

22	23	24		26
	33	34	35	36
42		44	45	46

	52		54	55	
61	62	63		65	66
71	72		74		76

61		63	64	65
71	72	73		
	82		84	

	76		78	79	
	86	87	88		90
95	96		98		100

Page 47 fell out of a book.
How would you tell a friend where it belongs?

____

Focus | Children fill in the missing numerals on pieces of 100-charts.

HOME CONNECTION
Show a page number between 50 and 100 from a book. Ask: "What is the next page number? What was the number on the page that came before? How do you know?"

Name: ______________________ Date: ______________________

Missing Number Mysteries

Fill in some numerals in this piece of a 100-chart.
Trade books with a friend.
Ask your friend to fill in the empty spaces.
Check your friend's work.

71									
									100

How did you choose the numerals to write in?

____

____

____

How did you know where to put the numerals you chose?

____

____

____

Focus | Children use a piece of a 100-chart to make a missing number puzzle for a friend to complete. Then, they check their friend's work.

Name: ______________________ Date: ______________________

100-Chart (101 to 200)

Circle numerals that show a pattern.
What is your pattern?

____

Colour numerals that show another pattern.
What is your pattern?

____

101	102	103	104	105	106	107	108	109	110
111	112	113	114	115	116	117	118	119	120
121	122	123	124	125	126	127	128	129	130
131	132	133	134	135	136	137	138	139	140
141	142	143	144	145	146	147	148	149	150
151	152	153	154	155	156	157	158	159	160
161	162	163	164	165	166	167	168	169	170
171	172	173	174	175	176	177	178	179	180
181	182	183	184	185	186	187	188	189	190
191	192	193	194	195	196	197	198	199	200

How are the patterns the same?

____

How are they different?

____

Focus | Children record and describe two number patterns on a 100-chart that shows 101 to 200.

Name: ______________________________ Date: ______________________________

Odd and Even Numbers

Colour the even numbers from 50 to 68 red.
Colour the odd numbers from 19 to 37 blue.

1	2	3	4	5	6	7	8	9	10
11	12	13	14	15	16	17	18	19	20
21	22	23	24	25	26	27	28	29	30
31	32	33	34	35	36	37	38	39	40
41	42	43	44	45	46	47	48	49	50
51	52	53	54	55	56	57	58	59	60
61	62	63	64	65	66	67	68	69	70
71	72	73	74	75	76	77	78	79	80
81	82	83	84	85	86	87	88	89	90
91	92	93	94	95	96	97	98	99	100

What patterns do you see?

____

____

____

Focus | Children colour a 100-chart to show odd and even numbers.

HOME CONNECTION

Have your child use the chart on this page to describe some number patterns on a 100-chart.

Name: ______________________ Date: ______________________

Counting Patterns

Look at each list of numbers.
What is the number pattern?

117,	118,	119,	120,	121	counting by ______
130,	140,	150,	160,	170	counting by ______
25,	50,	75,	100,	125	counting by ______
23,	25,	27,	29,	31	counting by ______

Find the patterns.
Write the missing numerals.

46,	48,	50,	___,	___,	___,	58,	___,	___,	64
25,	50,	75,	___,	___,	150,	___,	200,	___,	250
120,	130,	140,	___,	___,	170,	___,	___,	200,	___
95,	100,	105,	___,	115,	___,	___,	130,	___,	___

Focus | Children find and continue counting patterns.

Name: ____________________ Date: ____________________

Reaching 41

Will you reach 41 if you begin at 6 and count by 5s?
Show your thinking in pictures, numbers, or words.

Focus | Children use a number pattern to solve a problem.

Name: ______________________ Date: ______________________

Reaching 62

Will you reach 62 if you begin at 21 and count by 10s? Show your thinking in pictures, numbers, or words.

HOME CONNECTION

Have your child explain the clues in this problem and tell how he or she solved the problem.

Focus | Children use a number pattern to solve a problem.

Name: ____________________ Date: ____________________

How Many Paddles?

About how many paddles do you see?

Estimate. more than 50 fewer than 50

As you begin counting, look back at your estimate.

Change it if you want. _______

Show how you counted. Use pictures, numbers, or words.

There are _______ paddles in all.

Focus | Children estimate and count the number of paddles in a dragon boat race.

Name: ______________________ Date: ______________________

Dragon Boat Stories

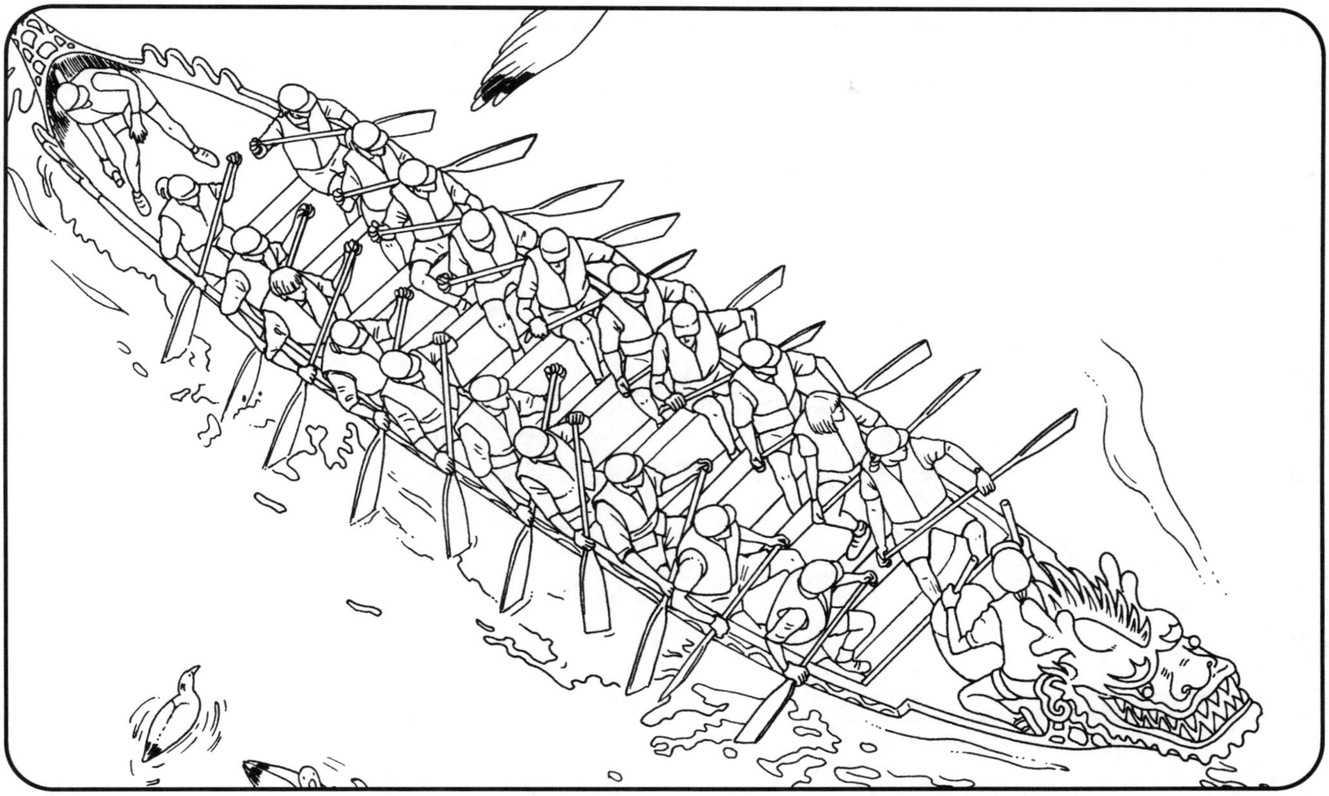

What is happening on the water?

Tell an addition story.

_____ + _____ = _____

Tell a subtraction story.

_____ − _____ = _____

Focus | Children interpret an illustration and write and solve addition and subtraction story problems.

Name: ______________________ Date: ______________________

My Journal

Tell what you learned about building numbers.
Use pictures, numbers, or words.

Tell what you learned about large numbers.

Focus | Children reflect on and record what they learned about number relationships.

HOME CONNECTION

Find out what your child learned about counting in this unit. Ask: "What is your favourite number? What are some different ways you can show it?"

UNIT 3

Time, Temperature, and Money

Focus | Children tell a story about the picture and discuss the duration and the order of events.

Name: ______________________ Date: ______________________

Dear Family,

In this unit, your child will be learning about time, temperature, and money.

The Learning Goals for this unit are to

- Name and order months and seasons of the year.
- Use ordinals *first* to *thirty-first*.
- Tell time to the quarter-hour on analog and digital clocks.
- Use a thermometer to see if the temperature is rising or falling.
- Count and create money amounts up to $1.00.

You can help your child achieve these goals by doing the Home Connection activities suggested at the bottom of selected pages.

Name: ______________________ Date: ______________________

Mixed-Up Apple Times

Look at the drawings.
Number the drawings in the order that they happen.

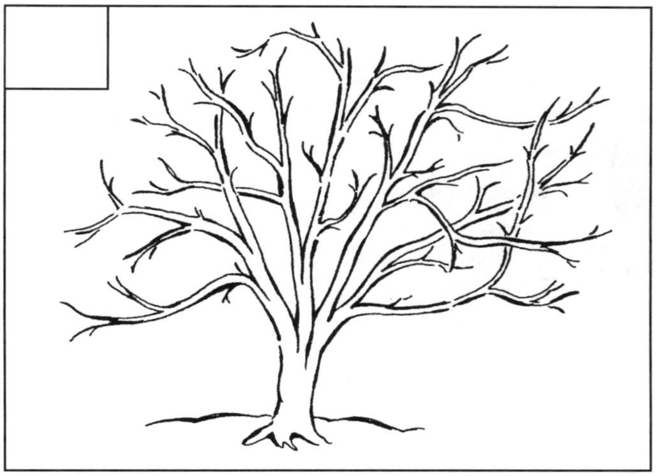

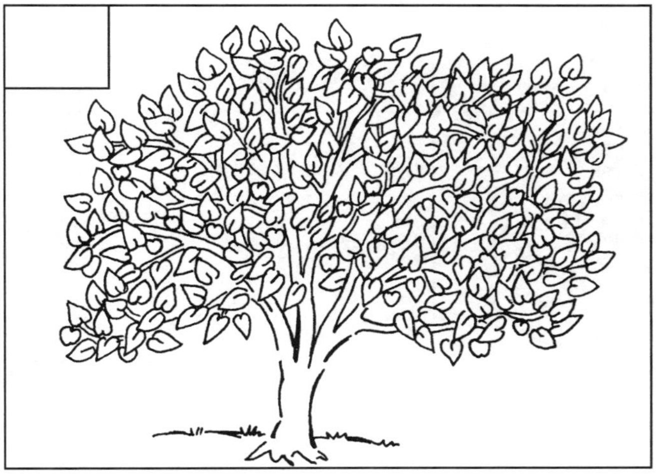

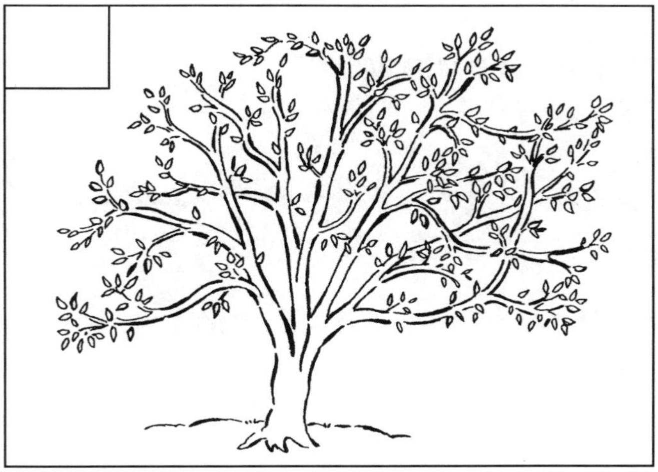

Write a story about the pictures. ______________________

____

____

____

____

FOCUS | Children order the pictures and create a story. There are multiple correct answers, depending on start position.

Name: ____________________ Date: ____________________

Counting Time

Count and record the number of swings each activity takes.
Add two more things to do, then count and record the swings.

Activity	Number of Swings
 Write your name.	
 Say the alphabet.	
 Draw a circle and colour it in.	

Focus | Children measure the duration of activities using a pendulum timer.

Name: ______________________ Date: ______________________

About Time

Estimate the number of swings each activity will take.
Time each activity. Record the number of swings.

Activity	Estimate	Count
Blink 10 times. 		
Draw a face. 		
Sing “Row, Row, Row Your Boat.” 		
Put on your coat. 		
Wash your hands. 		

HOME CONNECTION
Have your child explain how to use a pendulum to measure time.

Focus | Children estimate and measure the duration of activities using a pendulum timer.

Name: ______________________ Date: ______________________

How Long Is a Minute?

Count the number of times you can repeat each activity in one minute.

Activity	Number
Write your whole name.	☐
Draw a house.	☐
Make a 5-train with Snap Cubes.	☐

Focus | Children measure the number of repetitions that fill a minute.

Name: ______________________ Date: ______________________

Just a Minute

Write or draw pictures of 3 activities you think will take one minute.
Time how long each activity takes.

Circle the length of time for each activity.

Activity	
	less than a minute about a minute more than a minute
	less than a minute about a minute more than a minute
	less than a minute about a minute more than a minute

Focus | Children record activities they think will take one minute and then measure.

HOME CONNECTION

Ask your child to help you prepare a meal. Discuss what jobs will take one minute. Have your child check with a timer or a clock that has a second hand.

Name: ______________________________ Date: ______________________________

Hours, Minutes, Seconds, Days?

Decide whether each event should be measured in hours, minutes, seconds, or days.

the school day

____

blowing a bubble

____

walking a dog

____

eating dinner

____

FOCUS | Children decide what unit of time would be best to measure an event.

Name: ____________________ Date: ____________________

Time by 15

Show the time on each clock.

4:15

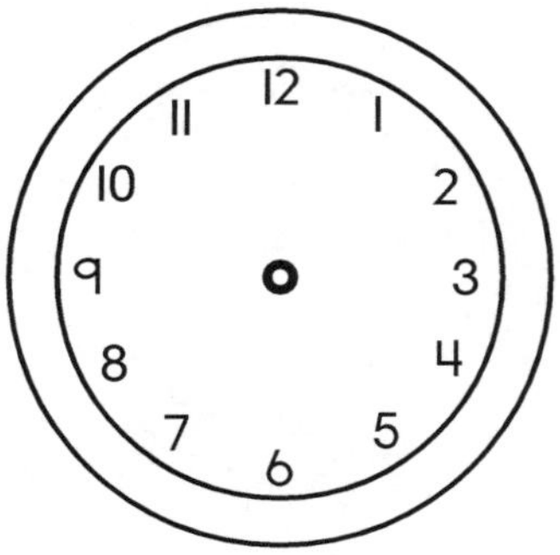

6:15

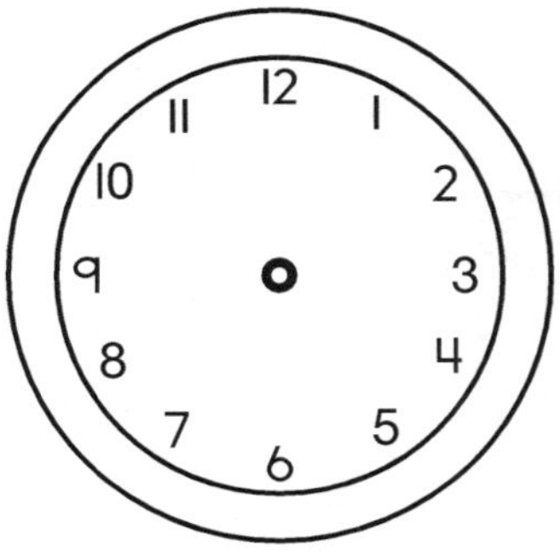

9:45

12:45

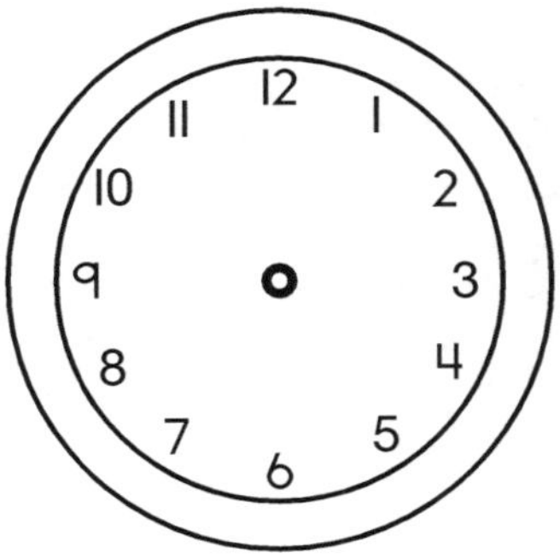

11:00

10:30

Focus | Children show time to the quarter-hour on analog clocks.

Name: ______________________ Date: ______________________

Telling Time

Write each time or show it on the clock.

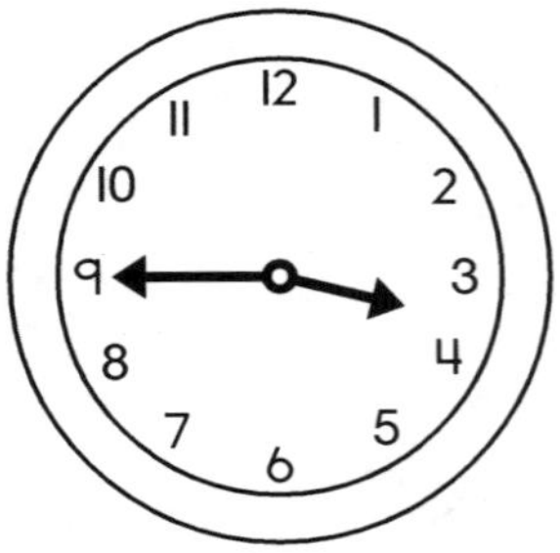

____

____

____

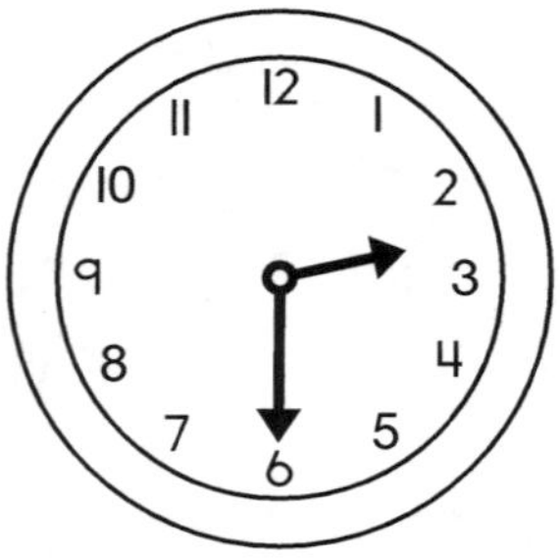

____

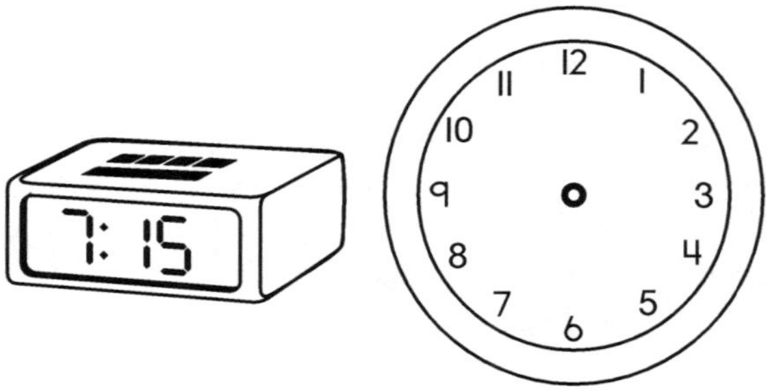

HOME CONNECTION

Make a book with your child to show the times of certain home events (for example: 8:30, leave for school; 6:15, time for supper).

Focus | Children record time to the quarter-hour using analog and digital clocks.

Name: ______________________ Date: ______________________

15 Minutes Later

The class is waiting for family day to start. Family members are invited to come at 11:00.

Beginning at 9:00, someone announces the time every 15 minutes.

Draw 6 times that are announced.

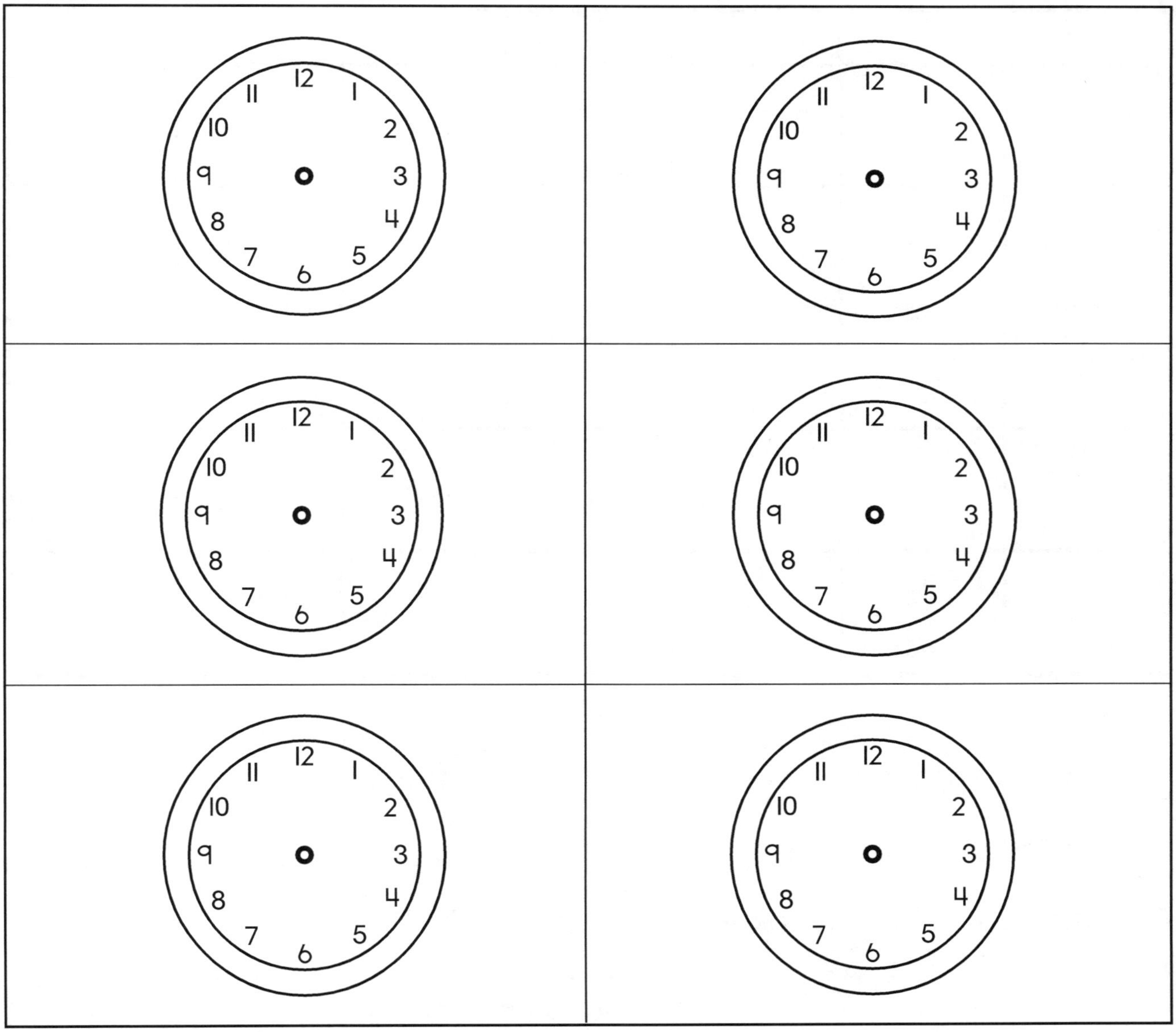

Focus | Children record quarter-hour intervals on analog clocks.

Name: ______________________ Date: ______________________

The Month of October

Look at a calendar for October.
Write the days of the week.
Write the numerals for the month.

October

How many weeks are in the month of October? ______

How do you know? ______________________

On what day of the week is the twenty-first? ______________________

HOME CONNECTION
With your child, discuss special events your family celebrates during a year. Have your child record these dates on a calendar.

Focus | Children read days and weeks on a calendar.

Name: ______________________ Date: ______________________

Calendars

Complete each calendar.

April

Sunday		Tuesday		Thursday		Saturday
		1	2		4	
	7	8		10		12
13		15			18	
			23		25	26
	28					

What day of the week is the fourteenth? ______________________

the sixteenth? ______________________

July

Sunday	Monday					Saturday
1		3		5		7
	9	10	11		13	
	16			19		21
22		24		26		
29						

What day of the week is the thirtieth? ______________________

the eleventh? ______________________

Focus | Children complete each calendar to show the days of the week and the dates in the month. They interpret the dates given ordinal clues.

Name: ______________________ Date: ______________________

Hot or Cold?

Colour to show the temperatures on the thermometers.

at the start

in hot water

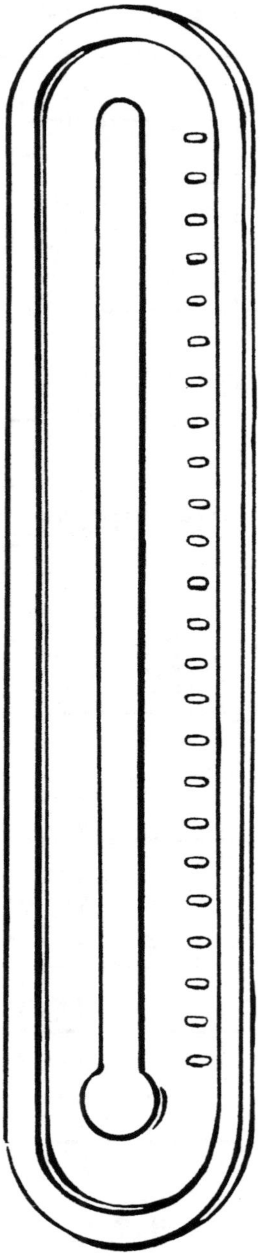

in cold water

HOME CONNECTION

Use a thermometer to test the temperature of a warm liquid, and then place the thermometer in a cup of cool water. Repeat with other warm and cool liquids. Ask your child what happens to the thermometer.

FOCUS | Children record rising and falling temperatures on the thermometer.

Name: ______________________ Date: ______________________

For Sale

Draw the coins you could use to buy each of these.

HOME CONNECTION

When shopping with your child, point out price tags on articles under $1.00 and have your child read the amount. Hand your child some change to count to determine if there is enough to buy an item.

Focus | Children count on and skip count to find the value of coins.

Name: ______________________ Date: ______________________

What Can I Buy?

You have 95¢.
Circle 3 things you could buy with that exact amount.
Show the coins you would use.

Could you buy 3 other things with that exact amount?
Show your work.

Focus | Children count on and skip count to find the total cost of 3 items.

Name: ______________________ Date: ______________________

Counting Coins

You have 6 coins that equal 90¢.
What could the coins be? Draw a picture of your solution.

HOME CONNECTION

Have your child explain the solution to the problem.
Ask: "How do you know the coins add up to 90¢?"

FOCUS | Children determine 6 coins that could have a total value of 90¢.

Name: ______________________________ Date: ______________________________

What Coins Would You Use?

What 6 coins would you use to make 75¢?
Use pictures, numbers, or words.

How do you know this makes 75¢?

____

Focus | Children determine what 6 coins they could use to make 75¢.

Name: ______________________ Date: ______________________

Sharing Money

Three children find 50¢ in coins.
How can they share the money?
Use pictures, numbers, or words.

Focus | Children use coins to show their solutions.

Name: ______________________ Date: ______________________

On Time

What time did the children leave for school?
Show the time on both clocks.

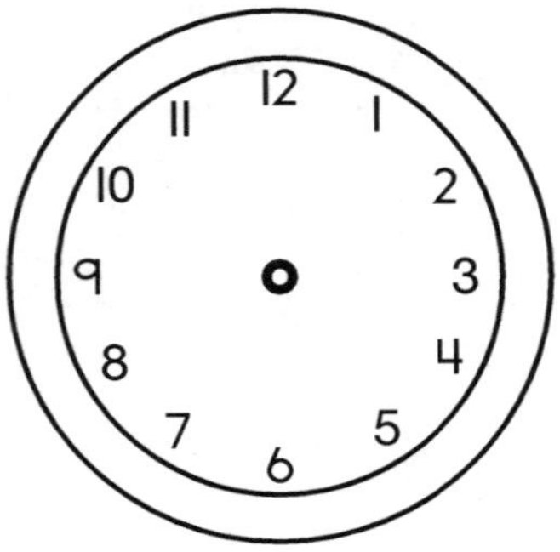

What time did school end?
Show the time on both clocks.

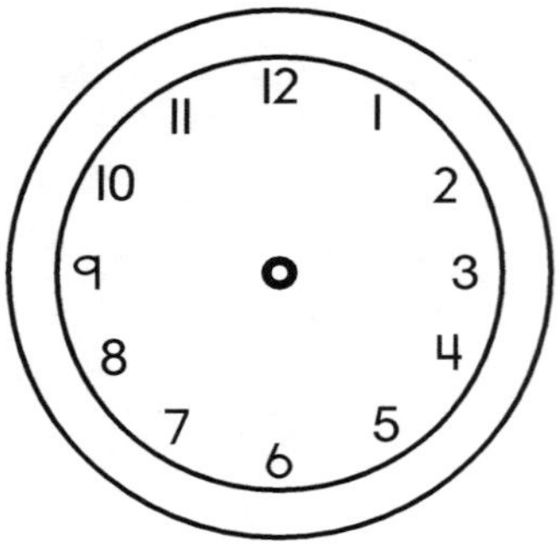

How is  the same as 

?

____

____

How are they different?

____

____

Focus | Children recall times to the quarter-hour from a story and record the times on digital and analog clocks.

Name: ______________________ Date: ______________________

Hotter, Colder

Show the temperatures during the day.

morning **noon** **late afternoon**

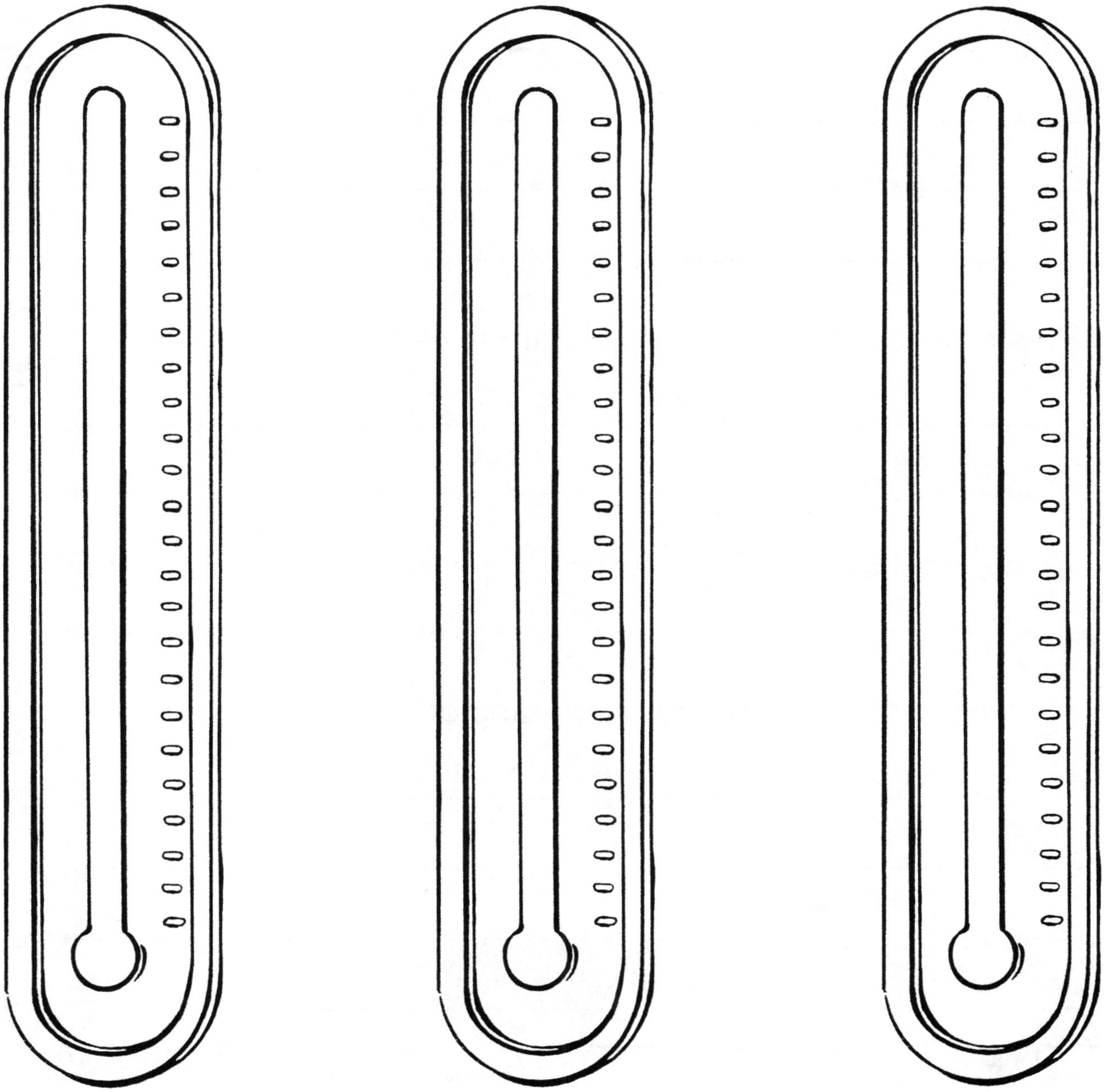

Focus | Children use colour to show relative temperatures on thermometers.

Name: ______________________________ Date: ______________________________

My Journal

Which clock do you prefer:  or 

?
Tell about your thinking.

____

____

____

____

How can you tell if the temperature is rising?

____

____

____

____

Tell what you learned about counting coins.

____

____

____

____

HOME CONNECTION

Invite your child to share what he or she liked about this unit.

Focus | Children reflect on what they have learned about time, temperature, and money.

The Skating Day

The class looked outside at the ice and the snow.
"If this storm doesn't stop soon, I don't think we'll go."
Then Cam's grandma came. "All the roads are okay.
We'll still take the bus to go skating today."

Take-Home Story

It was so frosty cold when they got on the bus,
they climbed on it quickly without any fuss.
Miss Chu called out names, as they passed her in line.
She didn't want any children left behind.

The volunteers helped them lace their skates on tight.
It was lots of hard work to tie them just right.
"It's freezing!" said Mishi. Her teeth loudly chattered.
"I love skating!" cried Cam. To him, nothing else mattered.

Once on the ice, it was easy to spot
the children who skated and those who did not.
Grandma flew by; she was spinning and turning.
She encouraged the children: "Once I was just learning."

Then Grandma stopped skating. "My scarf! Where's it gone?
I'm sure that this morning I put the scarf on."
They looked on the rink, but the scarf wasn't there.
They looked by the benches; they looked everywhere.

"Who'd want my scarf? That is puzzling to me."
Cam tugged Grandma's coat. Mishi said, "It was me.
I felt freezing cold, so I wrapped myself in it.
I thought I would borrow it just for a minute."

Grandma smiled. "I'm so glad that the scarf is not gone.
It's my favourite for winter, but you keep it on.
Let's skate a while longer, before leaving the rink.
Then, to warm up, we'll have hot chocolate to drink!"

About the Story

The story was read in class to prepare for a Mathematics Investigation activity. Children completed addition and subtraction activities, worked with number combinations, and counted in a variety of ways. They also identified and made their own patterns and used coins to represent different money amounts.

Talk about It Together

- What happens to Grandma's scarf while the class is at the ice arena?
- How do you think the parent volunteers might be using math during the field trip?
- How did Mishi feel when she realized she had the scarf?
- What kind of person is Grandma? Do you know someone like her? How is that person the same? Different?

At the Library

Ask your local librarian about other good books to share about patterning, numbers, and measuring time, temperature, and money.

How Can We Arrange 24 Children?

There are 24 children and 3 parts to the rink.
Show one way to arrange the children into 3 groups.

Show a different way to arrange 24 children in 3 groups.

Grandma's Scarf

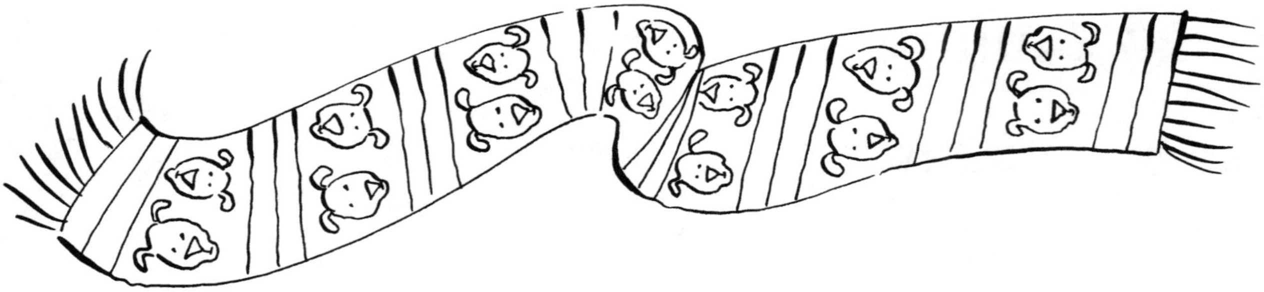

What is the pattern on Grandma's scarf?
Show the pattern, using 3 repeats.

Draw a circle around the pattern core.

Make your own pattern for a scarf.
Draw your pattern.

Describe your pattern.

How Many Skates?

Show 2 ways to count the skates.

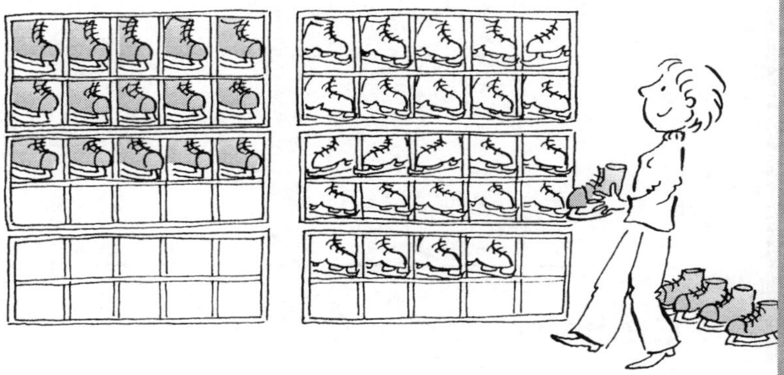

How many skates are there altogether? ______

Are there more hockey skates or figure skates?

____

How many more? ______

Show how you know. Use pictures, numbers, or words.

How many skates are needed for the children in your class?

Show your thinking. Use pictures, numbers, or words.

Buy Cam a Snack!

Grandma has $1.00 in coins.
Draw the coins that she could have in her purse.

Grandma can spend up to
$1.00 on Cam's snack.

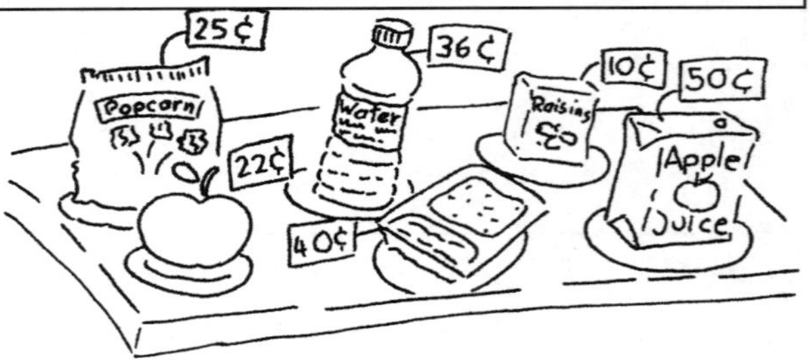

What can Grandma buy? ______________________________

____

How much will she spend? ____________
How much money will she have left?

Show another way she can spend the money. ___________

____

How much will she spend? ____________
How much money will she have left?

Floating Bubbles

Challenge a friend to see
whose bubble stays
in the air longer.
Blow at the same time
and begin counting slowly.

Do you think
you will get to 10? 20?
Will you get as high
as 50?

Food for Thought

Fill in the blanks with something that makes sense.

I could eat 100 ______________________

but not 100 ______________________.

I could lift 100 ______________________

but not 100 ______________________.

I would like to have 100 ______________________

but not 100 ______________________.

Make up some more sentences of your own.

 The next 4 pages fold in half to make an 8-page booklet.

Fold

Math at Home

**Hop aboard
the Math Express.
Where will we go today?
To a land of math mystery
where we can learn and play.**

**We'll see patterns and calendars
and numbers galore.
We'll see money and measuring,
so much fun in store!**

Math at Home I

Crazy Cookies

The cookie-making machine at a local factory has gone wild! Each time a cookie pops out, its shape changes. Check the first 3 cookies that came out.

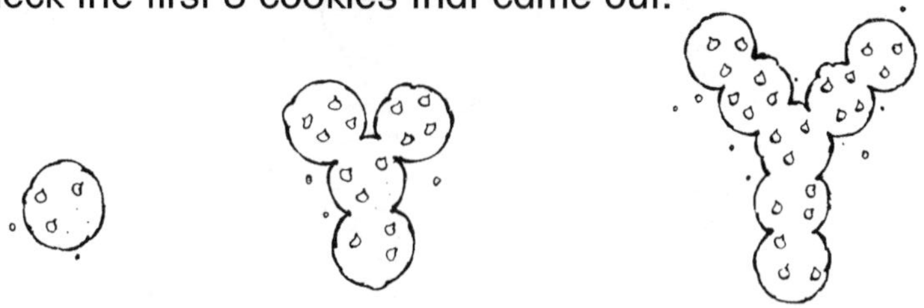

1st **2nd** **3rd**

What will the 5th cookie look like?
What will the 7th cookie look like?
Which one would you like to eat?

Find Your Page!

Find a book with a few hundred pages in it.
Get a friend to call out a page number that could be in the book.

Open the book as close as you can to that page number.
Estimate how far off you were, then give your friend a turn.

What was the closest you got?
Would it be easier if the book had 50 pages? Why?

Pattern Search

At home, look for patterns made with

- lines
- squares
- different shapes
- numbers

Can you find other types of patterns?

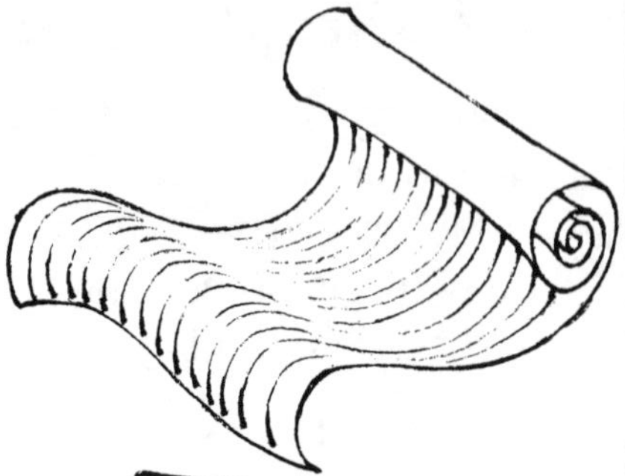

Elevating Elevators

Imagine you are in a really tall building.
You leave the doctor's office and get on the elevator at the 21st floor.
You need to go down 14 floors to get to the cafeteria.

Which button will you push?

Suppose you got on at the 17th floor and went up 18 floors.
On which floor will you get off?

Make up some elevator problems of your own.

Plenty of Time

Think of things you do every day and decide whether they take less than a minute, about a minute, or more than a minute to finish.

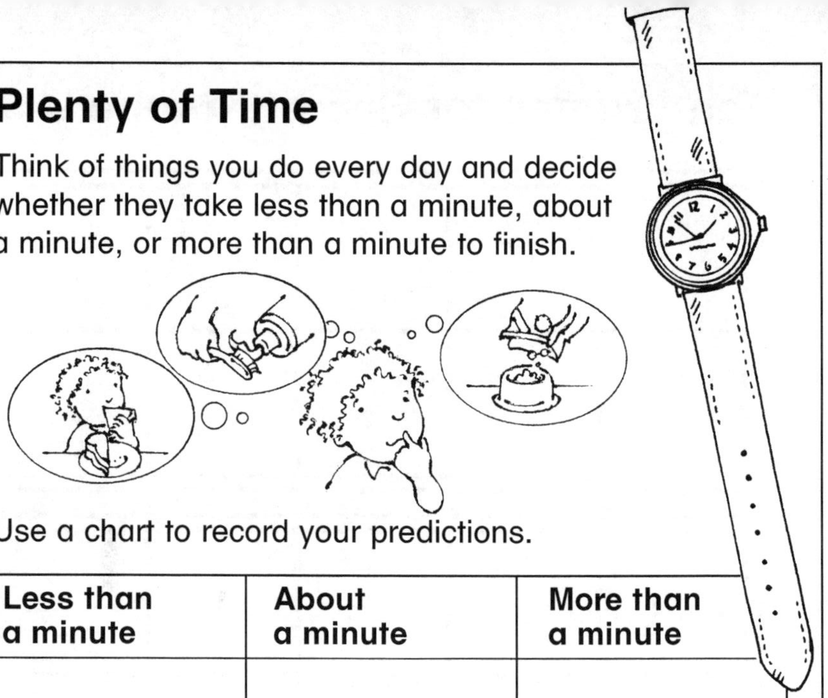

Use a chart to record your predictions.

Less than a minute	About a minute	More than a minute

All done? Put your list on the refrigerator. Next time you do one of the activities, check to see if your prediction was right!

When Were You Born?

Find out when each person in your family was born.
Whose birthday comes first in the year?
Whose birthday comes after yours?
Is there a month with more than one birthday?

Make a list or a picture to show what you found out.

Dirty Laundry

Max ran through a big puddle and then shook off the mud right beside the clean laundry.

Estimate how many mud spots landed on the sheet. (Think groups of 10s and the estimating will be a breeze!)

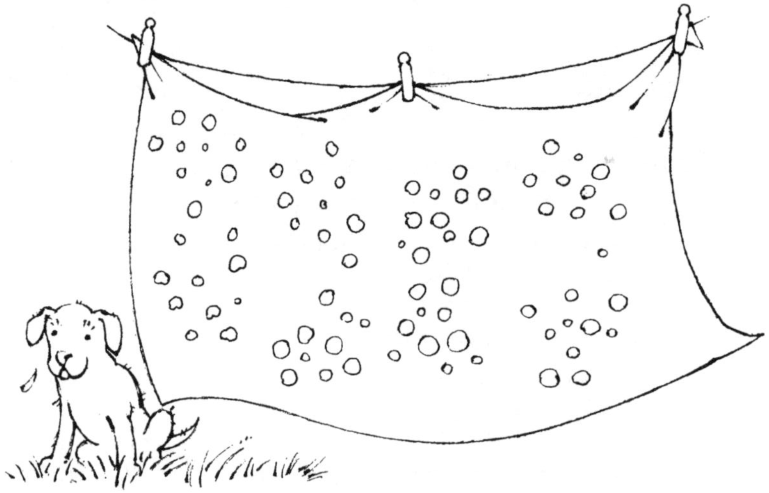

How Much Farther?

Next time you are in the car or on the bus, be on the lookout for place signs that show distance away in kilometres.
Which place is nearest?
Which is farthest?
How much farther?

Create other problems with these distances.

Secret Numbers

You'll need:
- 5 sets of number cards from 0 to 9, shuffled and placed face down
- ten-frames
- 20 counters

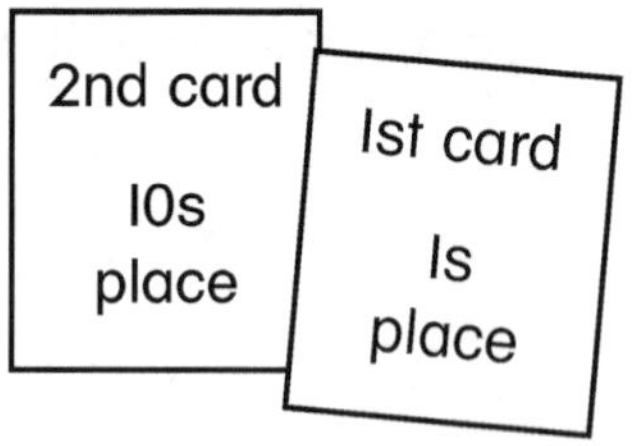

On your turn:
- Draw 2 cards and place them **face up** in front of you, like this.
- Draw 2 more cards and place them **face down** in front of a friend.

Your friend has a choice:
- Trade a card for one of yours.
- Leave the cards alone.

Once you trade or keep cards, look at the numbers.
- Flip over the face-down cards and then read both numbers.
- The player with the greater number puts a counter on his or her ten-frame.
- The cards go into the discard pile and the other player draws the next cards.

The first player to fill a ten-frame wins!

Ten-Frames for Secret Numbers

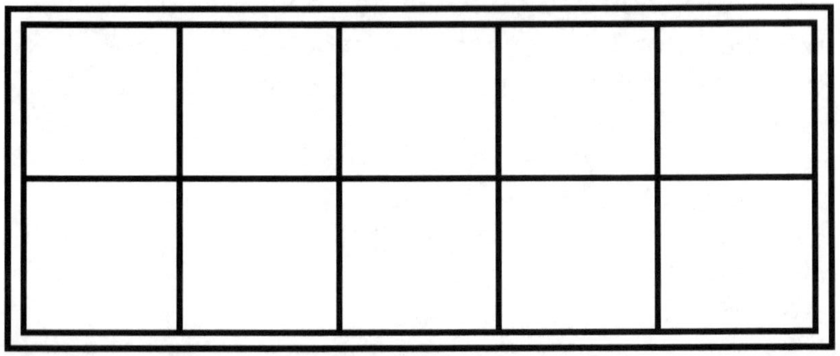

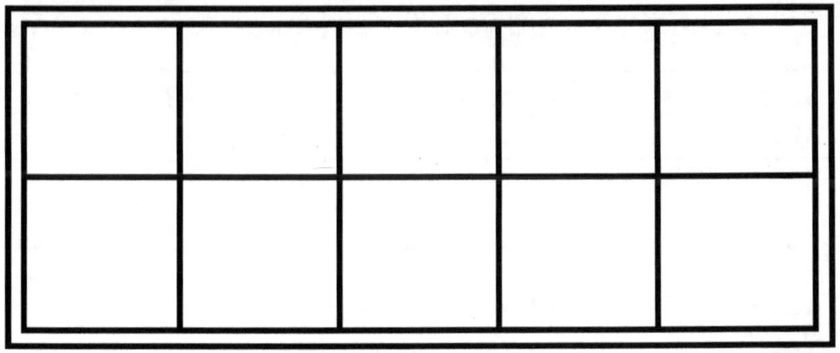

Can you think of a different game to play with the same materials?

UNIT 4

Exploring Addition and Subtraction

Focus | Children create number stories about a scene from a country fair.

Name: ______________________ Date: ______________________

Dear Family,

In this unit, your child will be developing strategies for adding and subtracting two-digit numbers.

The Learning Goals for this unit are to

- Add three addends (for example, 5 + 6 + 7 = 18).
- Use 10 to help when adding and subtracting.
- Add multiples of 10 to one- and two-digit numbers.
- Develop and use different strategies to add and subtract pairs of two-digit numbers.
- Look for patterns in digits when adding or subtracting.

You can help your child achieve these goals by doing the Home Connection activities suggested at the bottom of selected pages.

Name: ______________________ Date: ______________________

Number Stories from the Fair

Write two number sentences about each picture.

_____ + _____ = _____

_____ – _____ = _____

_____ + _____ = _____

_____ – _____ = _____

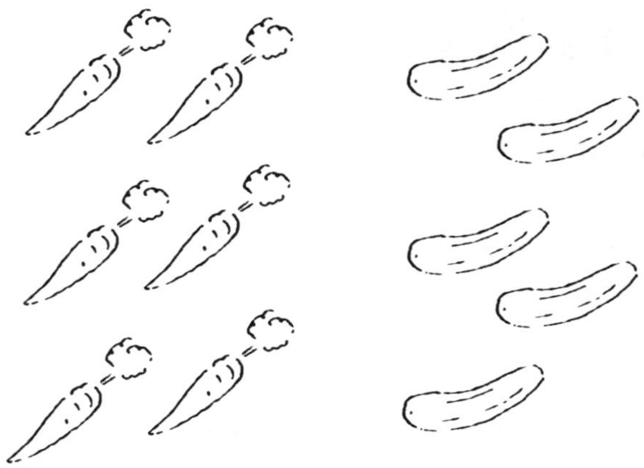

_____ + _____ = _____

_____ – _____ = _____

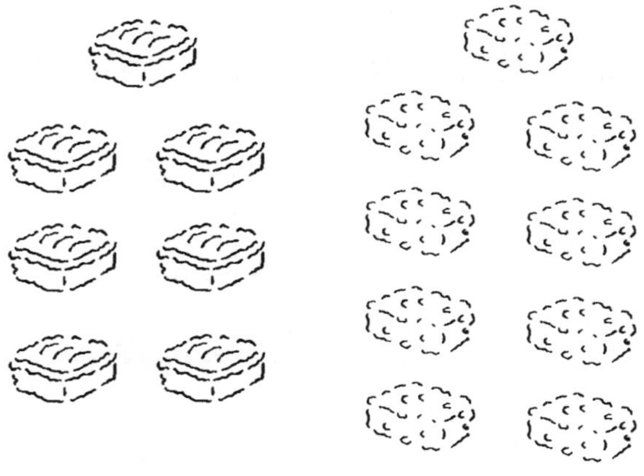

_____ + _____ = _____

_____ – _____ = _____

FOCUS | Children write addition and subtraction sentences about groups of items from a country fair.

Name: ____________________ Date: ____________________

Adding Rows and Columns

Look at the tables of numbers.
Add the numbers in each row.
Add the numbers in each column.

	column ↓	column ↓	column ↓	
row →	2	3	5	____
row →	8	2	7	____
row →	6	1	8	____
	____	____	____	

	column ↓	column ↓	column ↓	
row →	5	7	5	____
row →	7	3	2	____
row →	4	6	8	____
	____	____	____	

When did the "find 10" strategy help you?

____

____

When did the "near doubles" strategy help you?

____

____

What other strategies did you use?

____

____

____

HOME CONNECTION

Use the first three digits of phone numbers to write and solve addition sentences with your child. For example, if a phone number begins with 747, the sentence is 7 + 4 + 7 = 18.

Focus | Children use different strategies to add three numbers.

Name: ______________________ Date: ______________________

Adding Animals

Choose an animal group. Make an addition story.
Show how you solved the problem. Use pictures, numbers, or words.

Focus | Children add two-digit numbers using their own strategies.

Name: ____________________ Date: ____________________

Adding Your Way

The fair has a contest for the longest zucchini.
Omar grew a zucchini 43 cm long.
The winning zucchini is 11 cm longer.
How long is the winning zucchini?

Tell how you solved the problem.
Use pictures, numbers, or words.

There are 38 gasoline tractors in the tractor show.
There are 16 steam-powered tractors.
How many tractors are there altogether?

Tell how you solved the problem.
Use pictures, numbers, or words.

Focus | Children add two-digit numbers using their own strategies.

Name: ______________________ Date: ______________________

The Ferris Wheel

There are 28 people on the Ferris wheel.
45 more are waiting in line.
How many people are at the ride altogether?

Tell how you solved the problem.
Use pictures, numbers, or words.

Make up your own addition story.

_____ + _____ = _____

Focus | Children solve addition stories using their own strategies.

Name: ______________________ Date: ______________________

Find the Way Home

Help the cow find its way home to the barn.
Find each sum. Circle the pairs of numbers that add to 73.
Join the circled numbers to draw the path home.

64 + 9 = ____

56 + 9 = ____

57 + 17 = ____

50 + 23 = ____

27 + 18 = ____

40 + 23 = ____

42 + 31 = ____

37 + 25 = ____

32 + 41 = ____

43 + 30 = ____

62 + 10 = ____

28 + 45 = ____

Look at the pairs of numbers that add to 73.
Which sums were easy for you to find? Why?

____

____

Focus | Children add two-digit numbers using their own strategies.

HOME CONNECTION

Have your child explain how he or she found the answer to 64 + 9. Then, work together to think of three more pairs of numbers that add to 73.

Name: ______________________ Date: ______________________

Give Me 10

Choose a number between 1 and 9.
Write it as the starting number in the table below.
Add 10 to your number.
Write the sum in the first row of the table.
Use the sum as the starting number in the next row.
Add 10 each time. Keep going until you have filled all the rows.

Number	Add 10	Sum
	+ 10	
	+ 10	
	+ 10	
	+ 10	
	+ 10	
	+ 10	

What stays the same when you add 10 to a number?

____

What changes?

____

Predict what will happen if you add 10 three more times.

____

Check your prediction. Write the number sentences.

____ + ____ = ____   ____ + ____ = ____   ____ + ____ = ____

Focus | Children add 10 to a number several times and record the pattern.

Name: ______________________________ Date: ______________________________

Dime Addition

Add dimes to each bank.
Write the total amount of money in each bank.

_______¢ in all

_______¢ in all

_______¢ in all

_______¢ in all

_______¢ in all

_______¢ in all

HOME CONNECTION

Place 6 pennies in a row. Ask your child: "How many pennies are there?" Add a dime to the row and ask: "How much money is there altogether?" Continue adding dimes until you reach 96¢.

Focus | Children add dimes to find money amounts up to 99¢.

Name: ______________________ Date: ______________________

Adding 10s

Complete the addition sentences.

26 + 10 = _____ 81 + 10 = _____ 18 + 70 = _____

9 + 90 = _____ 31 + 40 = _____ 23 + 60 = _____

$$\begin{array}{r} 48 \\ +\ 30 \\ \hline \end{array} \qquad \begin{array}{r} 17 \\ +\ 60 \\ \hline \end{array} \qquad \begin{array}{r} 10 \\ +\ 40 \\ \hline \end{array} \qquad \begin{array}{r} 15 \\ +\ 50 \\ \hline \end{array}$$

$$\begin{array}{r} 29 \\ +\ 30 \\ \hline \end{array} \qquad \begin{array}{r} 11 \\ +\ 50 \\ \hline \end{array} \qquad \begin{array}{r} 16 \\ +\ 80 \\ \hline \end{array} \qquad \begin{array}{r} 12 \\ +\ 70 \\ \hline \end{array}$$

8 + 10 = _____ 13 + 30 = _____ 14 + 10 = _____

Suppose you add 20 to a number.
Predict how the number will change.

____

____

How can you check your prediction?

____

____

FOCUS | Children add groups of 10 to one- and two-digit numbers.

Name: ______________________ Date: ______________________

How Many Cakes?

The fair has an Ugly Cake contest for children.
There are 48 cakes entered in the contest.
Then, Mr. Melnik's class enters 6 more cakes.
How many cakes are there altogether?

Describe how you would find the answer.
Use pictures, numbers, or words.

Now, find these sums.

8	18	28	38
+ 6	+ 6	+ 6	+ 6

Look at all the sums on this page. How are they alike?

____

____

Predict the answer to 58 + 6. Add to check.

____

Focus | Children use their own strategies to find the sums of one- and two-digit numbers. Then, they find related sums and look for patterns.

Name: ______________________ Date: ______________________

Addition Patterns

Find the sums.

9	19	29	39	49	59
+ 5	+ 5	+ 5	+ 5	+ 5	+ 5
____	____	____	____	____	____

All the answers ____.

What is the answer to 79 + 5? ________

How do you know?

____

Find the sums.

4	4	4	4	4
+ 18	+ 28	+ 38	+ 48	+ 58
____	____	____	____	____

All the answers ____.

What is the missing number in 4 + ☐ = 92? ________

How do you know?

____

Focus | Children add one- and two-digit numbers and look for patterns in the sums.

HOME CONNECTION

Ask your child to explain how he or she found the missing number in 4 + ☐ = 92.

Name: ______________________________ Date: ______________________________

How Many More?

There are more cats than rabbits entered in the show. How many more? Show how you solved the problem. Use pictures, numbers, or words.

_____ − _____ = _____

Focus | Children look for information in a story and subtract two-digit numbers using their own strategies.

HOME CONNECTION

Work with your child to write a different subtraction-story problem using the information about the pet show.

Name: ______________________________ Date: ______________________________

To the Fair

There are 38 Grade 2 children going to a country fair.
Some Grade 1 children are also going.
Altogether, 62 children will go.
How many Grade 1 children are going?

Tell how you solved the problem.
Use pictures, numbers, or words.

Make up your own subtraction story.

_____ − _____ = _____

Focus | Children solve subtraction stories using their own strategies.

Name: ______________________ Date: ______________________

Left in the Line

There are 39 people lined up to ride the Rocket Blaster.
The ride ends and 16 people from the line get on.
How many are left waiting in the line?

Tell how you solved the problem.
Use pictures, numbers, or words.

Make up your own subtraction story.

_____ − _____ = _____

Focus | Children solve subtraction stories using their own strategies.

Name: ______________________ Date: ______________________

A Number Code

Ryan and Ayesha made up a code that uses numbers in place of letters. Here are some of the letters and numbers they use.

C	E	G	H	I	N	O	P	R	S	W
3	5	7	8	9	14	15	16	18	19	20

Ryan wrote these numbers: 16 9 7

What animal name do they spell? ______________

Ayesha wrote subtraction sentences as clues for her favourite farm animal. Solve each clue.

34 – 15 = _____ The letter is _____.

67 – 59 = _____ The letter is _____.

49 – 44 = _____ The letter is _____.

61 – 56 = _____ The letter is _____.

78 – 62 = _____ The letter is _____.

What is Ayesha's favourite farm animal? ______________

What animal name do these differences spell? ______________

22 – 19 = _____ 28 – 13 = _____ 55 – 35 = _____

Focus | Children subtract two-digit numbers using their own strategies to find encoded animal names.

Name: ______________________ Date: ______________________

How Many Now?

There are 56 children in the Fun Run.
9 children stop for a drink.
How many students are still running?

Describe how you would find the answer.
Use pictures, numbers, or words.

Now, find these differences.

$$\begin{array}{r} 16 \\ -\ 9 \\ \hline \end{array} \qquad \begin{array}{r} 26 \\ -\ 9 \\ \hline \end{array} \qquad \begin{array}{r} 36 \\ -\ 9 \\ \hline \end{array} \qquad \begin{array}{r} 46 \\ -\ 9 \\ \hline \end{array}$$

Look at all the differences on this page. How are they alike?

____

____

Predict the answer to 76 – 9. Then subtract to check.

____

Focus | Children use their own strategies to subtract one-digit numbers from two-digit numbers. Then, they find related differences and look for patterns.

Name: ______________________ Date: ______________________

Subtraction Patterns

68 - 6

Find the differences.

8	18	28	38	48	58
− 6	− 6	− 6	− 6	− 6	− 6
___	___	___	___	___	___

All the answers ______________________________.

What is the answer to 78 − 6? ________
How do you know?

____

Find the differences.

14	24	34	44	54
− 8	− 8	− 8	− 8	− 8
___	___	___	___	___

All the answers ______________________________.

What is the missing number in ☐ − 8 = 76? ________
How do you know?

____

Focus | Children subtract one-digit numbers from two-digit numbers and look for patterns in the differences.

HOME CONNECTION

Ask your child to explain how he or she found the missing number in ☐ − 8 = 76.

Name: ______________________ Date: ______________________

Feed the Pigs

Helping to feed the pigs is one of Hannah's farm chores. She puts ears of corn in buckets for them.

Bucket 1 has 37 ears. Bucket 2 has 41 ears. There are 95 ears of corn altogether. How many ears of corn are in Bucket 3?

Show how to solve the problem. Use pictures, numbers, or words.

Focus | Children use a problem-solving strategy of their choice to solve a story problem.

Name: ______________________________ Date: ______________________________

How Many Ears of Corn?

A farmer has 95 ears of corn.
The mother pig eats 46 ears.
One young pig eats 27 ears.
How many ears of corn does the other young pig eat?

Show how to solve the problem.
Use pictures, numbers, or words.

Focus | Children use a problem-solving strategy of their choice to solve a story problem.

HOME CONNECTION

Ask your child: "How can you check if your solution to the problem is correct?"

Name: ______________________ Date: ______________________

The Answer Is 53

Make 2 addition stories that have a sum of 53.
Use pictures, numbers, or words.
Write an addition sentence for each story.

_____ + _____ = 53

_____ + _____ = 53

Focus | Children demonstrate their understanding of addition by creating their own addition stories.

Name: ______________________________ Date: ______________________________

Subtraction Stories for 53

Make 2 subtraction stories that begin with 53.
Use pictures, numbers, or words.
Write a subtraction sentence for each story.

$53 - \_\_\_\_ = \_\_\_\_$

$53 - \_\_\_\_ = \_\_\_\_$

Focus | Children demonstrate their understanding of subtraction by creating their own subtraction stories.

Name: ______________________________ Date: ______________________________

My Journal

Tell what you learned about adding large numbers.
Use pictures, numbers, or words.

Tell what you learned about subtracting large numbers.
Use pictures, numbers, or words.

Focus | Children reflect on and record what they learned about different ways to add and subtract large numbers.

HOME CONNECTION

With your child, talk about situations at home when you would need to use addition or subtraction.

UNIT

5

Data Management and Probability

Always, Sometimes, Never!

Race to ten
is a game we will play.

I wonder which colour
will **likely** win today?

Tiles in a bag—
shake them all about.

Put your hand in
and pull one out.

Will it **sometimes** be yellow
or will it **never** be blue?

Will it **always** be red?
What is your clue?

Always, sometimes, never
are the words you will use.

Look at your tile and
record what you choose.

The first colour to ten
is the winner you see!

Always, sometimes, never—
what will it be?

Focus | Children predict and describe the outcome of a game.

Name: ______________________ Date: ______________________

Dear Family,

In this unit, your child will be learning about making graphs and probability—how likely an event is.

The Learning Goals for this unit are to

- Collect, organize, describe, and label data on graphs. For example, your child's class may tally the number of days there is rain, snow, sun, or clouds during a month and graph the results.
- Read graphs and ask questions about the data they gathered.
- Talk about probability in day-to-day situations using words such as *always*, *sometimes*, or *never* to describe events. For example: It sometimes snows in spring.
- Use mathematical language such as *likely*, *unlikely*, and *probably* when playing games. For example: I think the spinner will likely land on red.

You can help your child reach these goals by doing the Home Connection activities suggested at the bottom of selected pages.

Name: ______________________ Date: ______________________

Race to Ten

Which colour will win the race?
Circle your answer. **red** or **blue**

Game Directions

Place 10 red tiles
and 5 blue tiles in a bag.

Take a tile from the bag.

Colour one square on the path.

Put the tile back in the bag. Repeat.

Race to ten!

red										
blue										

Which colour won? ______________________

How do you know? ______________________________________

Why do you think that happened? ______________________________

____

Focus | Children pull a tile from a bag, colour a square on the path, replace the tile, and repeat until one row is filled.

Name: ______________________ Date: ______________________

Build the Snow Pictures

Choose a spinner.
Circle your choice. 

Print **A** on one part of the spinner.
Print **B** on the other part.

You will spin 10 times.
Which snowperson will **likely** be taller, **A** or **B**?

Spin 10 times.
Which snowperson was taller? Why do you think that happened?

Choose a different spinner. 
Play again.

Which snowperson do you think will be taller, **A** or **B**?

Which snowperson was taller? Why do you think that happened?

FOCUS | Children build cut-out pictures from *LM 6: Build the Snow Pictures* according to spinner outcomes.

Name: ______________________ Date: ______________________

The Tortoise and the Hare Race

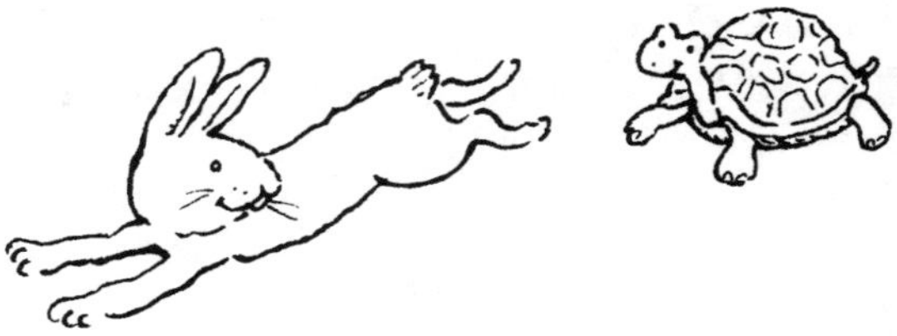

Choose a spinner.
Circle your choice. 

Print **T** for **tortoise** on one part.
Print **H** for **hare** on the other part.

Who do you think will win?
Spin the spinner. Colour one square for each spin.

Tell what happened. ____

____

Choose a different spinner. 
Play again.

Who do you think will win?
Spin the spinner. Colour one square for each spin.

Tell what happened. ____

____

Focus | Children choose and label a spinner from *LM 5: Spinners*, predict the winner, and record results.

Name: ______________________ Date: ______________________

Likely or Unlikely?

Look at each picture. Circle likely or unlikely.

likely unlikely

likely unlikely

likely unlikely

likely unlikely

likely unlikely

likely unlikely

Make Your Own likely

unlikely

Focus Children look at the picture and decide whether it is likely or unlikely. They create their own likely and unlikely pictures.

HOME CONNECTION

Make a likely/unlikely book with your child. Fold paper in half and have your child draw likely events on one side and unlikely events on the other.

Name: ______________________ Date: ______________________

Make a Game

Which spinner will you use in your game?
Circle it. 

What do the players try to do in your game?

What will **probably** happen if each player spins 10 times?
Tell about your thinking.

Play your game with a partner. Tell what happened.

Focus | Children design a game with a spinner, predict the results, and play the game, explaining the results.

Name: ______________________ Date: ______________________

Change the Spinner

Play your game again.
Choose a different spinner.

Circle it. 

Predict what will **probably** happen
when you play your game using this spinner.

Tell about your thinking.

Play your game with a partner. Tell what happened.

Focus | Children predict what will happen if they use a different spinner to play their game and explain the results.

Name: ______________________ Date: ______________________

Make a Bar Graph

Toss a two-coloured counter 15 times.

Predict which colour will come up most often.
Circle **red** or **yellow**.

Make a tally chart.

Colours	**Tally**
red	
yellow	

Make a bar graph to show the results.

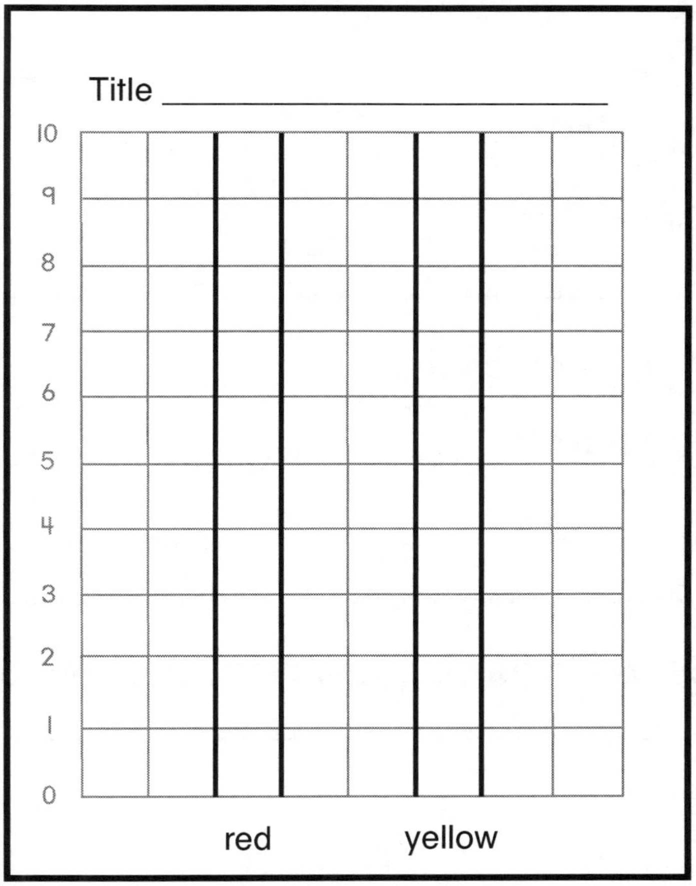

What did you find out?

____

____

____

Focus | Children predict the results of tossing a two-colour counter, and record results in a tally and on a bar graph.

Name: ______________________ Date: ______________________

Tally and Count

I counted all the chairs in our classroom.

My tally is ______________________.

There are ________ chairs.

I counted all the ______________________ in our classroom.

My tally is ______________________.

There are ______________________.

I counted all the ______________________ in our classroom.

My tally is ______________________.

There are ______________________.

How did tallying help you with your counting?

Focus | Children make a tally of different items in the classroom.

Name: ______________________ Date: ______________________

A Fishy Graph!

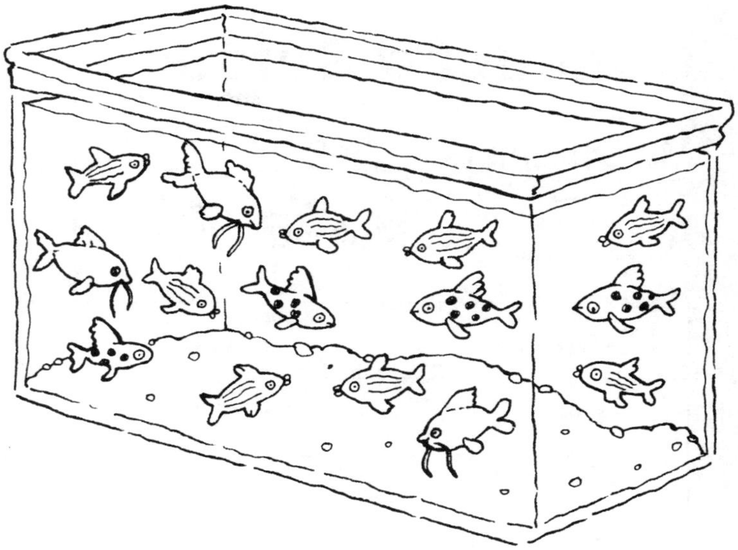

How many fish have stripes?
How many fish have spots?
How many fish have whiskers?

Make a tally chart.

Type	Tally
stripes	
spots	
whiskers	

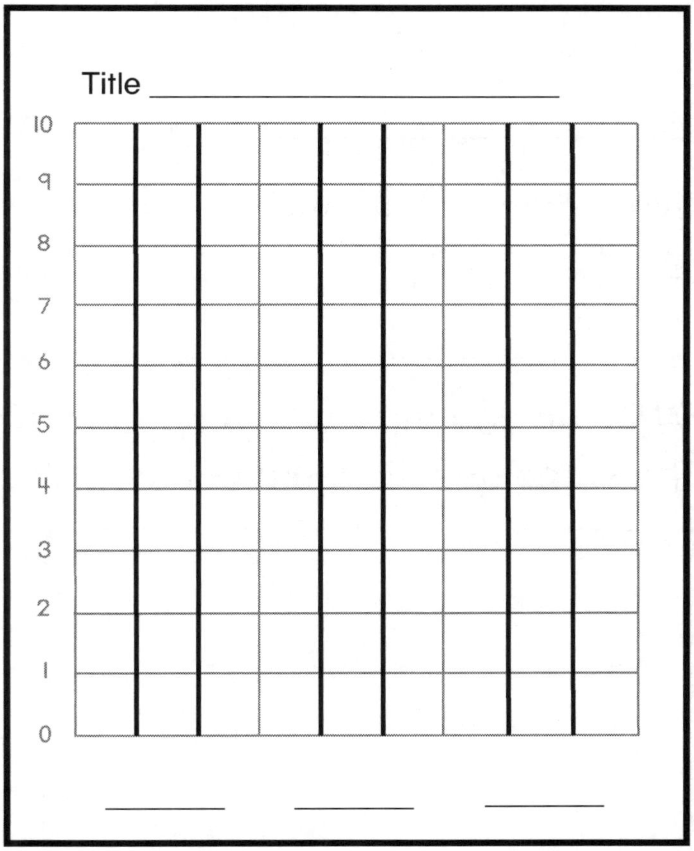

Make a bar graph to show the results.

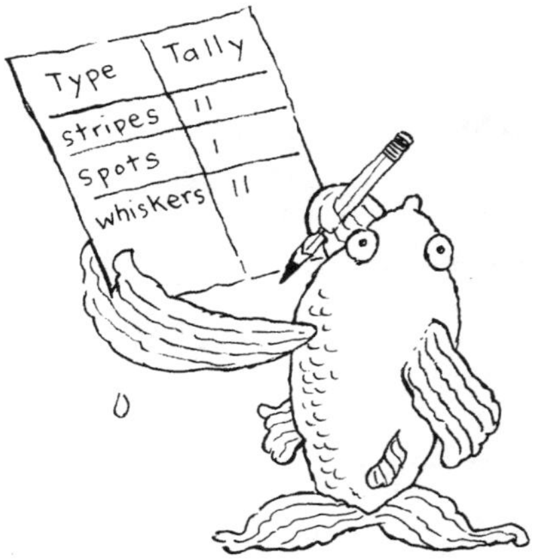

Write a true statement about the fish.

____

HOME CONNECTION

Practise making a tally at home with your child, for example, by tallying all the spoons in the drawer, or the books on a shelf.

Focus | Children make a bar graph to show how many fish there are of each type.

Name: ______________________ Date: ______________________

Conduct a Survey

My Question ______________________

Ask 10 friends. Make a tally chart.

Choices	Tally

What did you find out?

____

____

What do you think would happen if you asked the same question in a Grade 5 class?

HOME CONNECTION

Have your child ask a question of the family, such as: "Do you like the snow?" Have your child ask up to 10 family members or friends, then make a tally and bar graph of the results.

Focus | Children conduct a survey and record the results in a graph.

Name: ____________________ Date: ____________________

What Is Your Favourite?

My Question

Do you like __________, ____________, or ___________ the best?

Ask 10 friends. Make a tally chart.

Types of Food	Tally

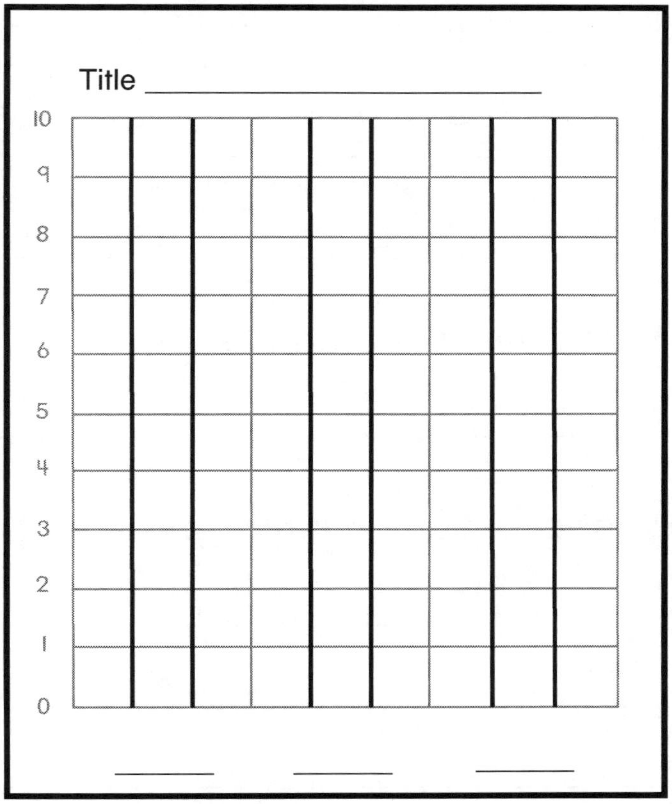

Make a bar graph to show the results.

What did you find out? ______________________________

____

What did you learn about conducting a survey?

____

____

Focus | Children conduct a survey and display the results in a bar graph.

Name: ______________________ Date: ______________________

Dinosaur Graph

Ari's Toy Dinosaurs

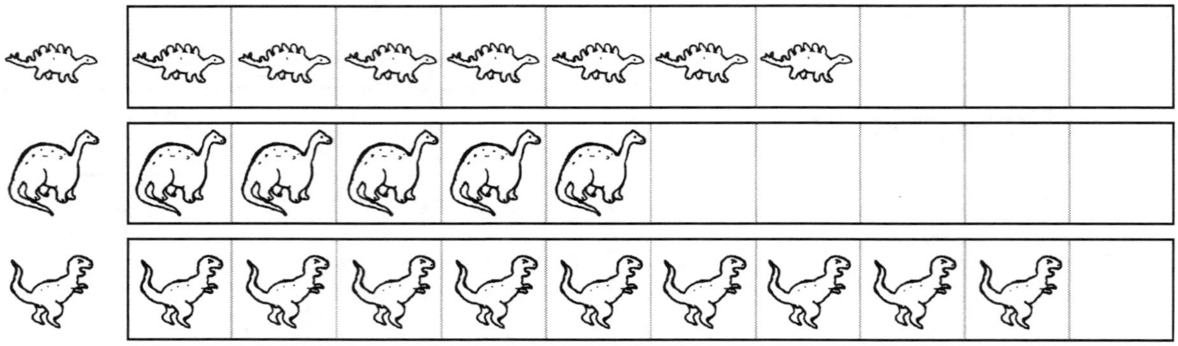

What does this graph tell you?

____

What questions can you ask about it?

____

____

____

What did you learn from this graph?

I learned that ______________________________________

____

I learned that ______________________________________

____

Focus | Children read and interpret a graph about dinosaurs and ask questions about the graph.

Name: ______________________ Date: ______________________

At the Park

Do you like to go to the park?

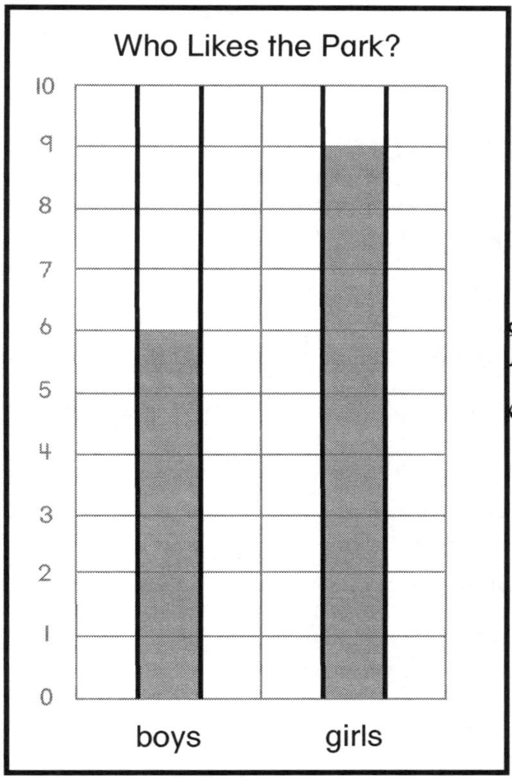

What is the graph about? How do you know?

____

____

One question I have about the information is

____

____

FOCUS | Children read and interpret a bar graph. They ask a question about the information shown.

Name: ______________________________ Date: ______________________________

Greater or Less?

Before you play the game, predict.
Will most sums be greater or less than your number?

Circle **greater** or **less**.

Explain your thinking in pictures, numbers, or words.

Make a graph on the next page to show your results.

Did your results match your predictions? **yes** **no**

Make 2 true statements about your results.

____

____

If you play the game again, what do you think will happen?
Use pictures, numbers, or words to explain why.

Focus | Children choose a number between 9 and 15, then turn over two cards and record whether the sum is greater or less than their number. They continue until they have used all of the cards; then they graph the results.

Name: ______________________ Date: ______________________

Our Results

Play "Greater or Less?"
Make a tally chart.

Sums	Tally
sums less than ____	
sums of ____	
sums greater than ____	

Make a bar graph to show the results.

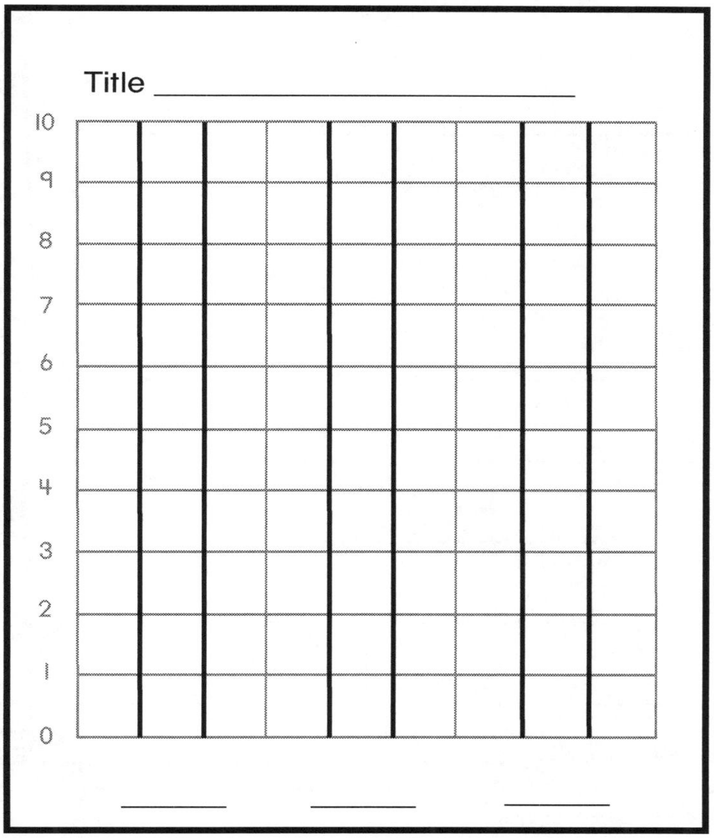

HOME CONNECTION

Use game board number cubes to play a game with your child. Even or odd? Roll the number cubes, and find the sum. If it's odd, one player gets a point. If it's even, the other player gets a point.

Focus | Children create a tally and bar graph to display the results of their "Greater or Less?" game.

Name: ______________________ Date: ______________________

My Journal

Tell what you have learned about spinners and how they work.

____

____

____

____

____

____

What are graphs used for?

____

____

____

____

____

Focus | Children use pictures, numbers, or words to reflect on what they have learned about data management and probability.

UNIT 6

3-D Geometry

Focus | Children identify and describe geometric solids.

Name: ______________________ Date: ______________________

Dear Family,

In this unit, your child will be learning about 3-D objects, such as cubes, spheres, cylinders, prisms, and pyramids.

The Learning Goals for this unit are to

- Describe, compare, and sort 3-D solids according to their attributes, such as whether they roll or stack, have curved or flat surfaces.
- Use 3-D solids in constructions.
- Make skeletons to represent 3-D solids.
- Use language such as *pyramid, prism, face,* and *edge* to describe solids.

You can help your child achieve these goals by doing the Home Connection activities suggested at the bottom of selected pages.

Name: ______________________ Date: ______________________

Our Construction

We made a ______________________ .

We used these solids.

Solid	How Many Solids?
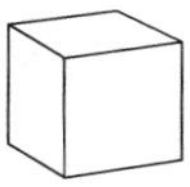	

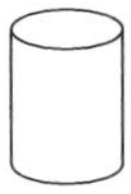	
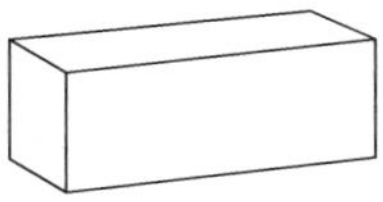	

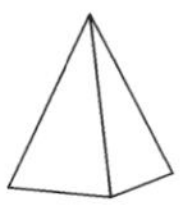	

We used ________ solids in all.

Focus | Children construct a 3-D model of a building and record the number of each type of solid they used.

Name: ______________________ Date: ______________________

A Sorting Rule

Make a sorting rule.

My sorting rule is ____

____.

Circle the objects that fit your rule.

What other way can you sort the solids?

Write another sorting rule. ______________________________________

____

Put an ✘ on the objects that fit your new rule.

Focus | Children create two sorting rules and identify objects in the picture that fit each rule.

Name: ______________________ Date: ______________________

Solids That Are Alike

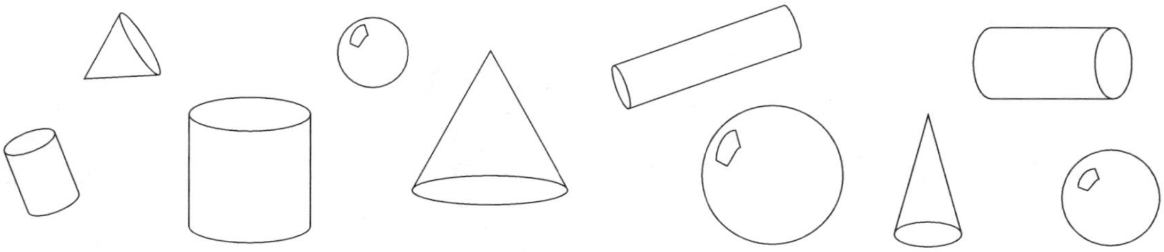

All these solids have ______________________.

They can all ______________.

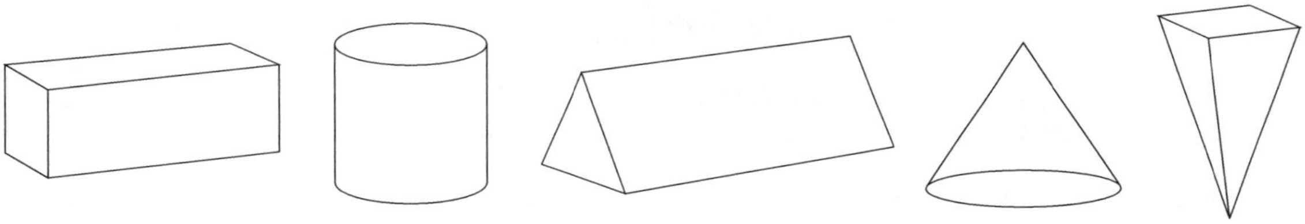

All these solids have ______________________.

They can all ______________.

In which group would you put a cube? Explain.

____

____

HOME CONNECTION

Ask your child to think of an object that can be added to the first group and explain his or her choice. Repeat the activity for the second group.

FOCUS | Children identify shared attributes for groups of objects.

Name: ______________________ Date: ______________________

Same and Different

What solid did your teacher give you?

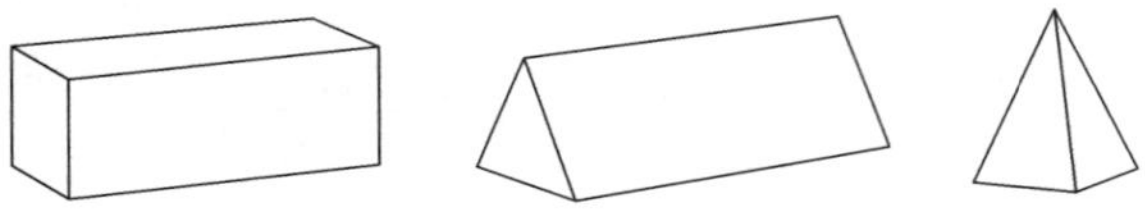

Circle it. Underline its name in the chart.

Choose another solid.

Circle it. Underline its name in the chart.

Count the faces, edges, and vertices on your solids. Fill in the chart.

	Rectangular Prism **Triangular Prism** **Pyramid**	**Cone** **Cylinder** **Sphere** **Cube**
Number of Faces		
Number of Edges		
Number of Vertices		

How are the two solids the same? ______________________

____

How are they different? ______________________

____

Focus | Children record the numbers of faces, edges, and vertices in each of two solids. Then they compare the solids according to their attributes.

Name: ______________________ Date: ______________________

How Many Faces?

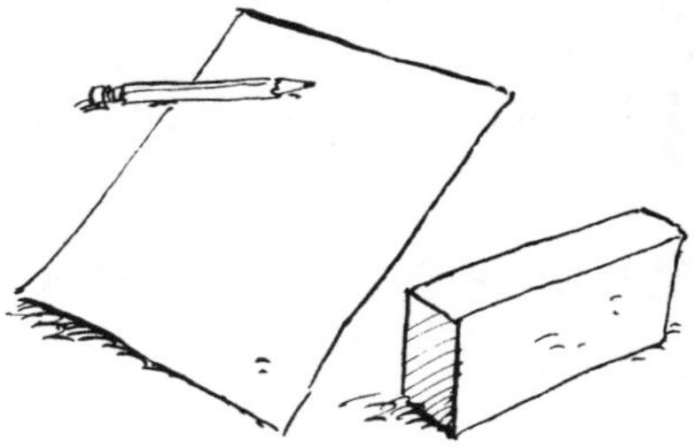

A  has 5 faces.
Draw the faces you traced.

How many 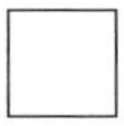 faces? ________ How many  faces? ________

A 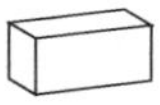 has 6 faces.
Draw the faces you traced.

How many  faces? ________ How many 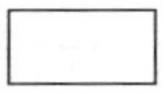 faces? ________

How are the two solids alike?

____

How are they different?

____

Focus | Children trace around the faces of two solids and identify the number of each type of face. Then they compare the solids.

Name: ______________________ Date: ______________________

Use the Clues

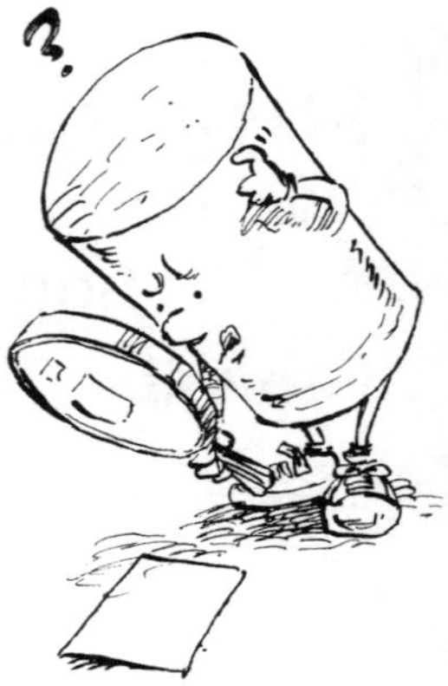

Use geometric solids like these.

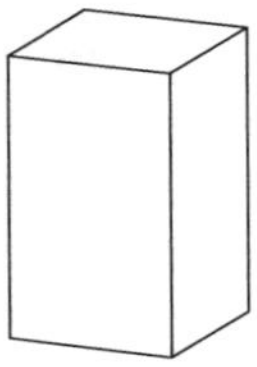

rectangular prism

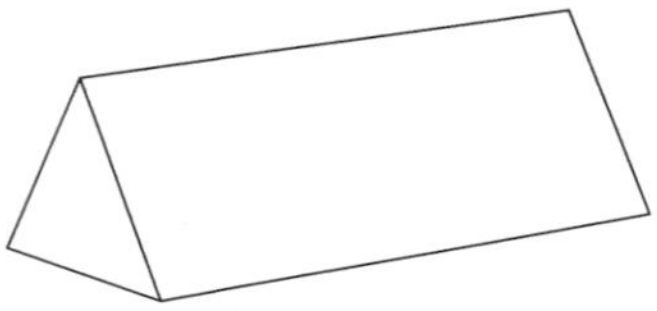

triangular prism

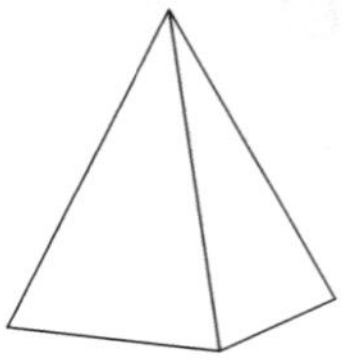

pyramid

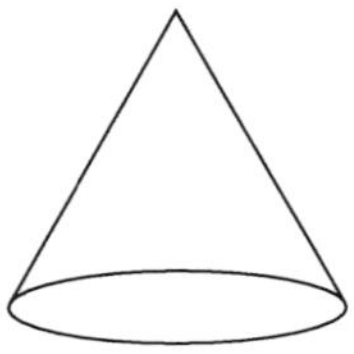

cone

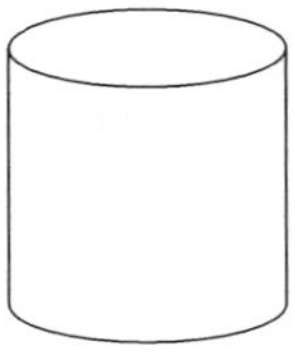

cylinder

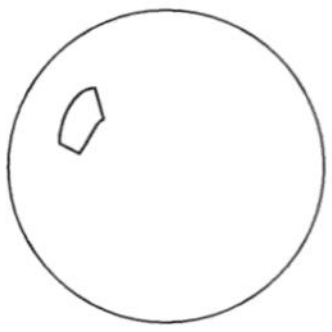

sphere

Follow the clues to fill in the chart.

Clue	**Solid**
greatest number of faces	
only one vertex (point)	
two circular faces	
five vertices (points)	
two triangle faces	
no vertices (points)	

HOME CONNECTION

With your child, hunt for objects that are examples of cubes, rectangular prisms, triangular prisms, and pyramids. Have your child choose two objects and tell how they are the same and how they are different.

Focus | Children use clues about faces, edges, and vertices to identify 3-D solids.

Name: ______________________ Date: ______________________

The Construction Challenge

Circle the structure you are going to build.

- the widest structure
- a castle with at least one pyramid
- a structure with only prisms
- the strongest structure
- a structure with a ramp
- the tallest structure
- a structure with exactly eight solids
- a lookout tower
- a structure with two cylinders
- a structure that uses one of each of the solids

Build your structure.

Tell how you made your structure.
Use pictures, numbers, or words.

Focus | Children choose a structure to build and then explain how they built it.

Name: ____________________ Date: ____________________

The Best House

Which house would you choose?
Circle your choice.

Explain your choice. ______________________________

____

Show how to build the house using solids.
Use pictures, numbers, or words.

Focus | Children choose their favourite house from three pictures. They explain their choice and tell how to build it with solids.

HOME CONNECTION

Gather boxes, paper-towel rolls, and funnels. With your child, take turns building different structures (for example, a tall tower or a structure using at least six objects). Think aloud as you work so your child can listen to how you solve problems.

Name: ______________________________ Date: ______________________________

Modelling Clay Solids

Which picture did you choose?
Circle it.

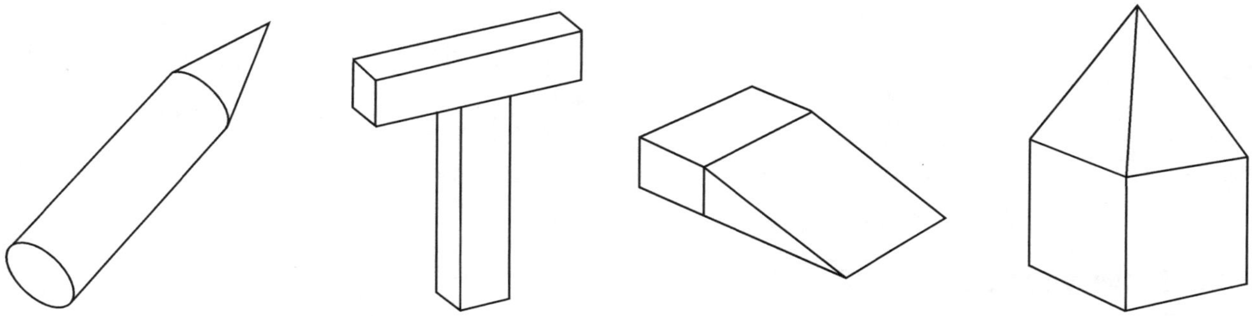

How did you use solids to make your model?
Use pictures, numbers, or words to explain.

Focus | Children explain how they created a model for a structure pictured on *Big Math Book, page 29.*

Name: ______________________ Date: ______________________

Making Solids

Use modelling clay to make one of these solids.

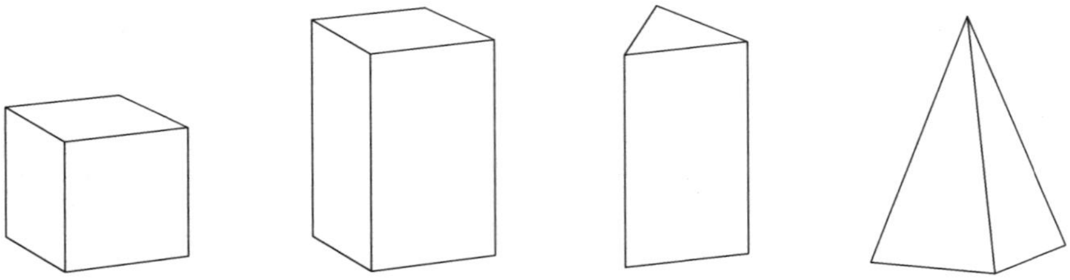

Show how you made your solid.
Give tips that would help a friend make it.

Use pictures, numbers, or words.

Which solids are best for building? Why? ______________________

____

Focus | Children construct a solid from modelling clay and explain how they did it.

Name: ______________________ Date: ______________________

See the Solids

How many pyramids and prisms do you see?

	Number of Rectangular Prisms	**Number of Triangular Prisms**	**Number of Pyramids**
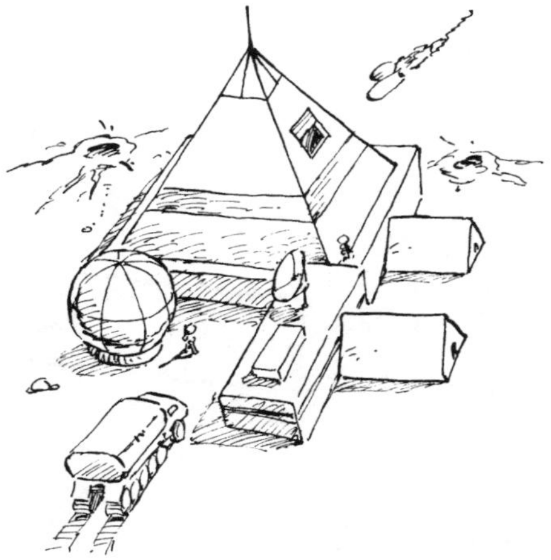			

Focus | Children count and record the number of rectangular prisms, triangular prisms, and pyramids they see in the illustrations.

HOME CONNECTION

Have your child work with modelling clay to practise making various solids. Ask how many faces, edges, and corners your child sees for each solid.

Name: ______________________ Date: ______________________

Skeletons

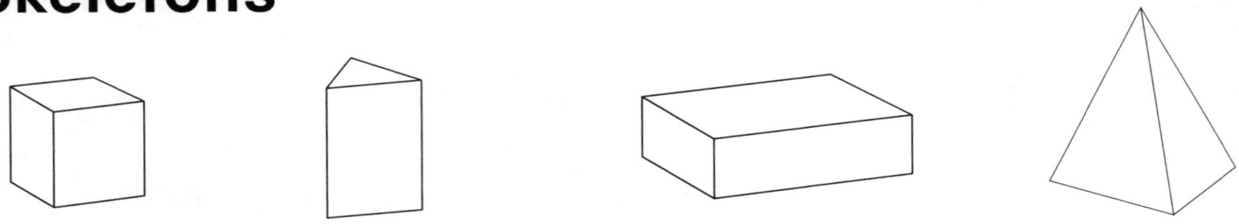

cube | triangular prism | rectangular prism | rectangular pyramid

Match each skeleton to a solid.

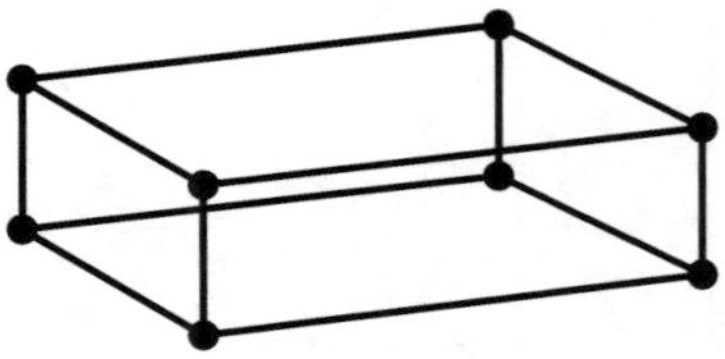

This is the skeleton of a ____________________.

How do you know? ____________________

____

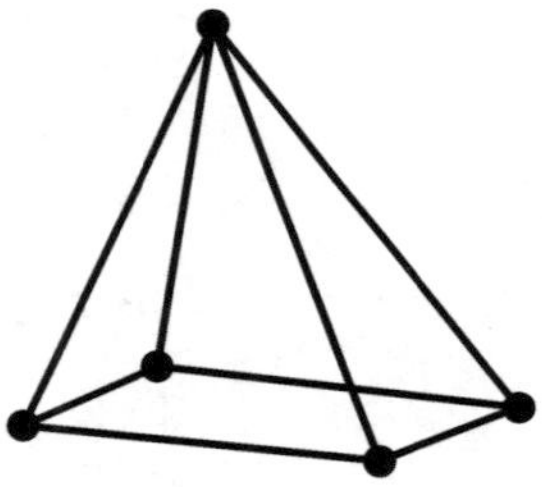

This is the skeleton of a ____________________.

How do you know? ____________________

____

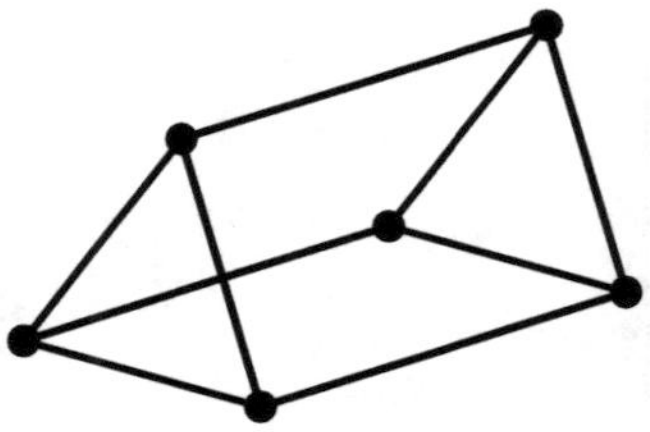

This is the skeleton of a ____________________.

How do you know? ____________________

____

Focus | Children name the solid represented by each skeleton model and explain their thinking.

Name: ______________________ Date: ______________________

Build a Skeleton

Use straws and clay to build a skeleton.

I built a skeleton for a ______________________.

How many did you use?

I used ________ long straws.

I used ________ short straws.

I used ________ pieces of clay.

Write two tips for building the skeleton.

1. ____

____

____

2. ____

____

____

A ______________ cannot be built as a skeleton.

Why? ____

HOME CONNECTION

Ask your child: "What steps did you use to build the skeleton?"

Focus | Children use straws and clay as joiners to build a skeleton. They then give tips for building the skeleton.

Name: ______________________________ Date: ______________________________

How Many for a Cube?

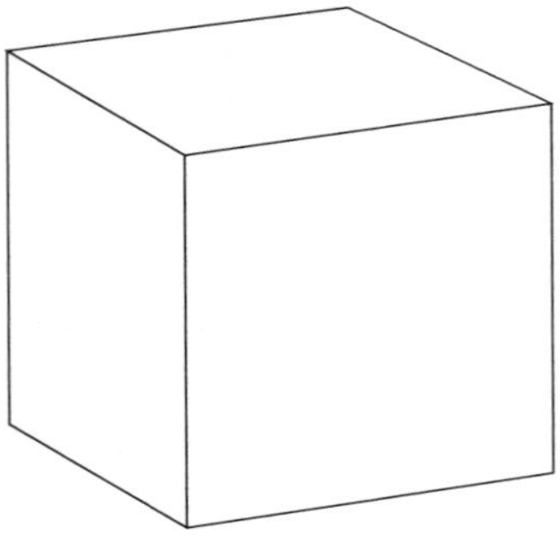

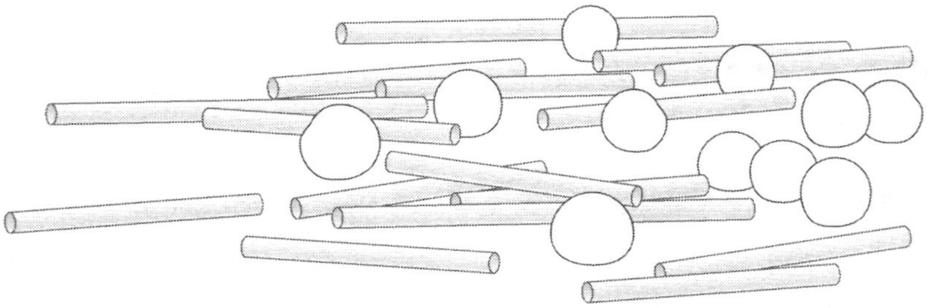

Plan to make a skeleton for a cube.

How many straws and pieces of clay will you need?

Fill in the chart.

Solid	**Number of Straws**	**Number of Pieces of Clay**
cube		

Tell how you solved the problem. Use pictures, numbers, or words.

Focus | Children determine how many straws and pieces of clay as joiners they need to build the skeleton of a cube. Then they record how they solved the problem.

Name: ______________________________ Date: ______________________________

How Many for a Prism or a Pyramid?

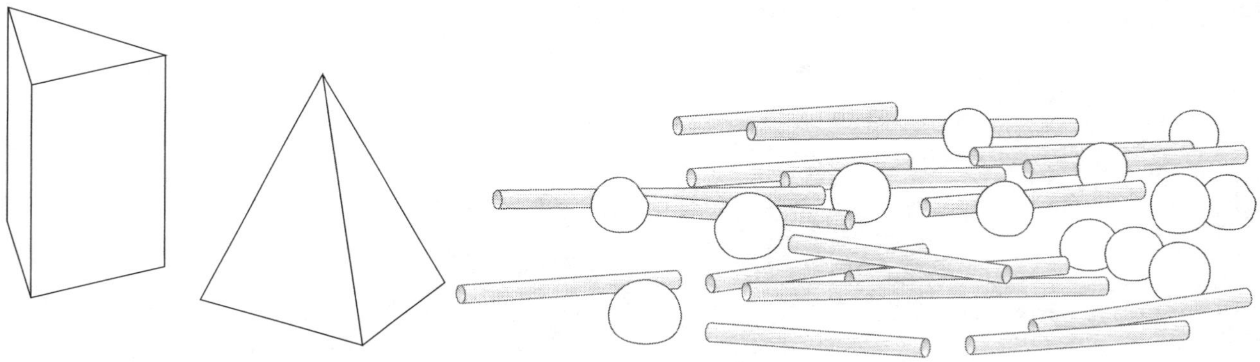

Choose one solid.

How many straws and pieces of clay will you need to make its skeleton?

Fill in the chart.

My Solid	Number of Long Straws	Number of Short Straws	Number of Pieces of Clay

Tell how you solved the problem. Use pictures, numbers, or words.

Focus | Children determine how many straws and pieces of clay as joiners they need to build the skeleton of a solid. Then they record how they solved the problem.

Name: ______________________ Date: ______________________

Pack the Spaceship

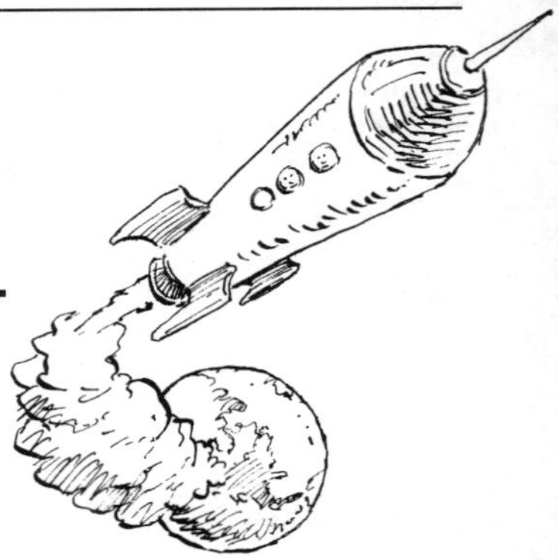

The astronauts are taking these supplies on their trip.

The astronauts need to pack the supplies in three bins.

Choose a sorting rule for each bin.
Decide which objects to put in.

Circle the objects that go in Bin 1.
The objects go together because they all have ________________.

Write an ✘ on objects that go in Bin 2.
The objects go together because they all have ________________.

Place a ✔ on objects that go in Bin 3.
The objects go together because they all have ________________.

FOCUS | Children sort objects into three bins and explain their reasoning.

Name: ______________________ Date: ______________________

Build a Spaceship

Which solids will you need to build this spaceship?

Make them from modelling clay.
Put them together to match the picture.

Think of another structure you can build.
Use solids to make it.

How many solids did you use? ______________________

Solid	Number of Solids in the Spaceship	Number of Solids in My Structure
cube		
rectangular prism		
triangular prism		
pyramid		
cone		
cylinder		
sphere		

Focus | Children build two structures and record how many of each type of solid they used in their structures.

Name: ______________________ Date: ______________________

My Journal

Tell about the spaceship and the structure you built.
Use pictures, numbers, or words.

What did you learn about solids?
Use pictures, numbers, or words to show your thinking.

HOME CONNECTION

Invite your child to help put away groceries. Talk about why you place particular packages or supplies together.

Focus | Children tell about their spaceship and the structure they built. Then they relate what they learned about 3-D solids in the unit.

UNIT 7

Addition and Subtraction to 100

FOCUS | Children identify the different ways to show 67.

Name: ______________________ Date: ______________________

Dear Family,

In this unit, your child will be learning about addition and subtraction of two-digit numbers, and developing an algorithm for finding and recording solutions.

The Learning Goals for this unit are to

- Model addition and subtraction of two-digit numbers on a place-value mat.
- Use the standard algorithm as one way to add and subtract two-digit numbers.
- Pose and solve number problems requiring addition or subtraction.
- Use a calculator to solve addition or subtraction problems with numbers over 50.

You can help your child achieve these goals by doing the Home Connection activities suggested at the bottom of selected pages.

Name: ______________________ Date: ______________________

Take a Number

Choose a number from the team line-up. Circle it.

Show your number at least 2 ways.

Choose another number. Put a square around it.
Compare this number to your first choice.
Use pictures, numbers, or words.

Find 2 numbers that come between your numbers.

____

Focus | Children represent a number in different ways, and compare numbers.

HOME CONNECTION

If your child has a collection of objects at home – stickers, stuffed toys, rocks, models – gather some together and ask your child to count the collection in at least 2 different ways.

Name: ______________________ Date: ______________________

Same Number, Different Ways

Choose a two-digit number.
Model the number on a place-value mat.
Draw a picture of your place-value mat.

_____ 10s _____ 1s __________ in all

Use the same two-digit number.
Model the number a different way on a place-value mat.
Draw a picture of your place-value mat.

_____ 10s _____ 1s __________ in all

Focus | Children choose a two-digit number and represent it with Snap Cubes and ten-sticks in multiple ways.

Name: ______________________ Date: ______________________

Make a Match

Look for matching place-value mats.
Join each pair by drawing a line.

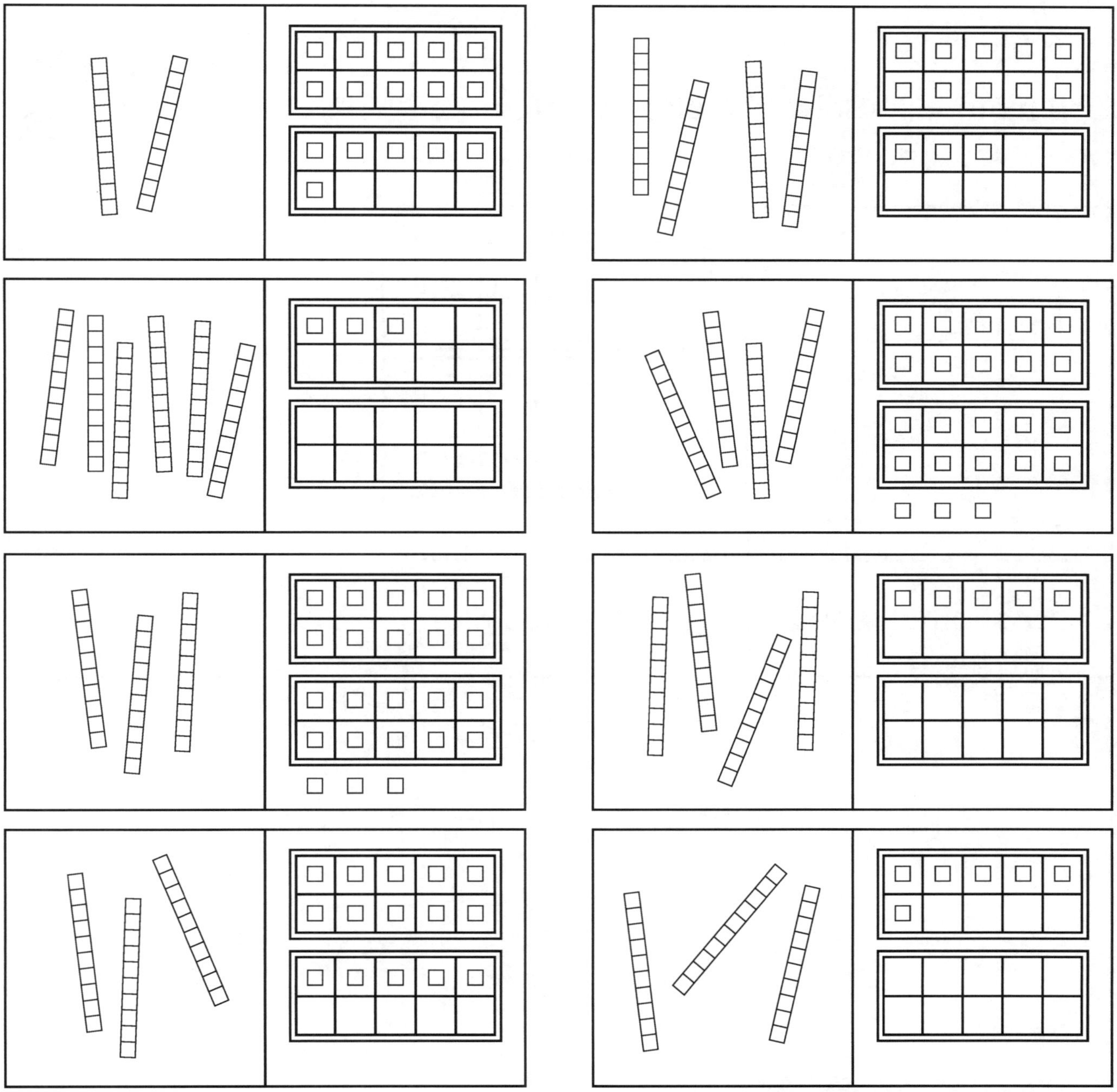

HOME CONNECTION

Make paper clip or elastic band chains to represent 26 (2 chains of 10 and 1 chain of 6). Ask your child to write the number in 3 ways.

Focus | Children identify equivalent representations of numbers displayed on place-value mats.

Name: ______________________ Date: ______________________

On with the Show!

The Grade 2 children put on a show.
They gave out 28 blue tickets.
They gave out 37 yellow tickets.
How many tickets did they give out in all?

Use materials. Solve the story problem.
Show your answer.

Show another way to solve the problem.

Focus | Children use base ten concepts and materials to solve an addition problem.

Name: ______________________ Date: ______________________

At the Show

The Grade 2 show was held in the gym.
The children helped to bring 55 chairs to the gym.
They still need 25 chairs.
How many chairs do
they need altogether?

Use materials.
Solve the story problem.
Show your answer.

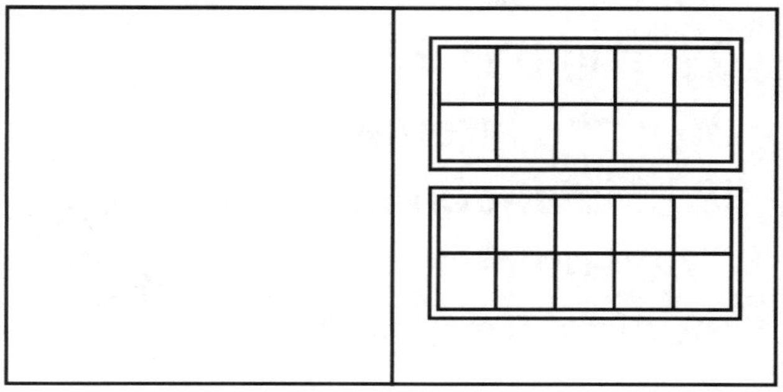

The Grade 2 children served refreshments after the show.
Jordan poured cups of lemonade.
Kiya handed out 24 cups of lemonade.
18 cups of lemonade
were still on the table.
How many cups of lemonade
did Jordan pour?

Solve the story problem.
Show how you solved it.

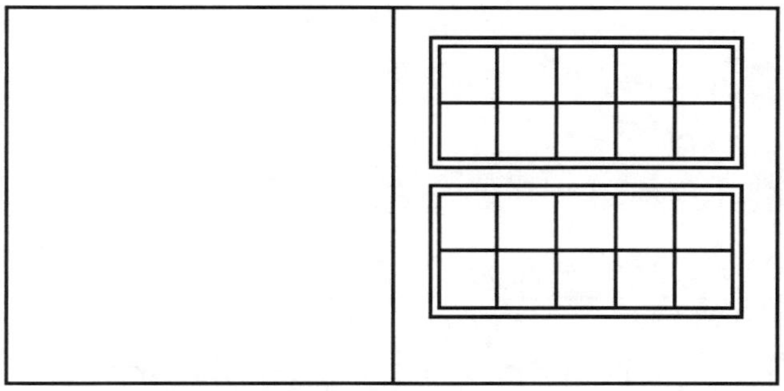

Make your own story problem. Solve it.

____

____

____

____

Focus | Children create and solve story problems involving addition, using place-value concepts.

Name: ______________________ Date: ______________________

Clean-Up Time

After the show, the Grade 2 children helped clean up.
There were

28 red balloons
28 blue balloons
36 white streamers
18 blue streamers
37 clean cups
43 dirty cups

Make a story problem about the Grade 2 clean-up.
Solve your problem. Show your work in pictures, numbers, or words.

Make another story problem.
Change books with a partner. Solve your partner's problem.

Partner's Name

____

Focus | Children create and solve story problems involving addition, using place-value concepts.

Name: ______________________ Date: ______________________

It All Adds Up

Which addition sentences do you think will need a trade?
Circle them.

Use materials and a place-value mat.
Answer the addition problems you circled.

22 + 23 = _____	67 + 26 = _____	53 + 20 = _____
9 + 40 = _____	34 + 57 = _____	19 + 49 = _____

Write the problems that do not need a trade.
Solve them.

____

____

How did you know which problems needed a trade?

____

____

FOCUS Children identify addition problems that require trading, or renaming a number, and use materials to find the sums.

HOME CONNECTION
Provide straws or toothpicks that can be clustered into 10s with a twist tie. Ask your child to model one of the addition problems from this page.

Name: ____________________ Date: ____________________

How Many Shells?

Laura collects shells.
She has 36 shells.
She finds 28 more on the beach.
How many shells does Laura have?

Build the addition story on a place-value mat.
Record it here.
Then record the addition using numbers.

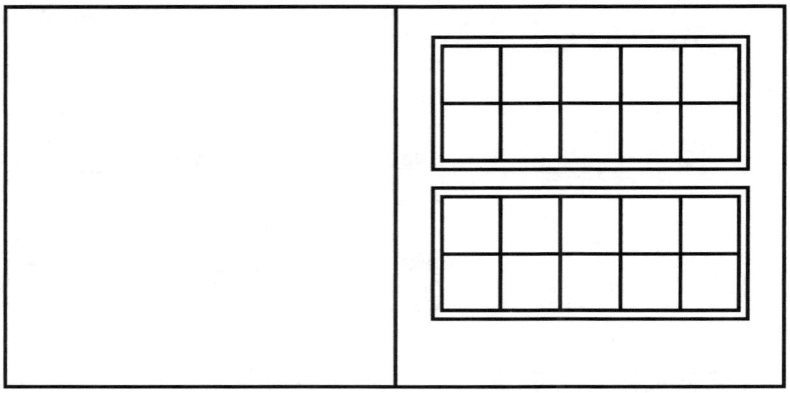

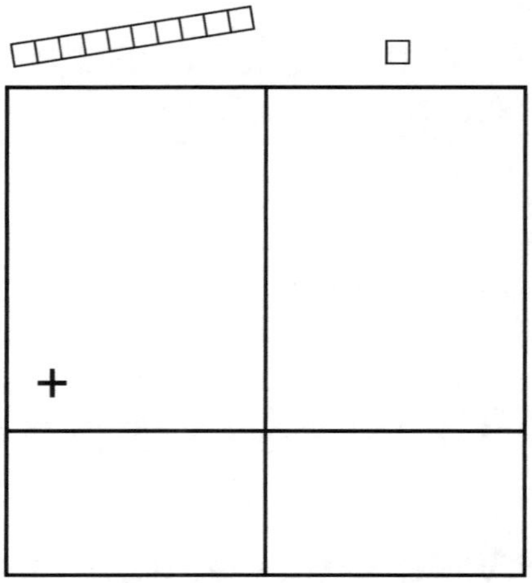

How are the two ways of finding the answer the same?

____

____

How are they different?

____

____

Focus | Children use materials to solve an addition problem using the standard algorithm, and record their work.

Name: ______________________ Date: ______________________

In the Schoolyard

There are 37 children in the schoolyard.
The bus arrives with 25 more children.
How many children are in the schoolyard now?

Build the addition story on a place-value mat.
Record it here.
Then record the addition using numbers.

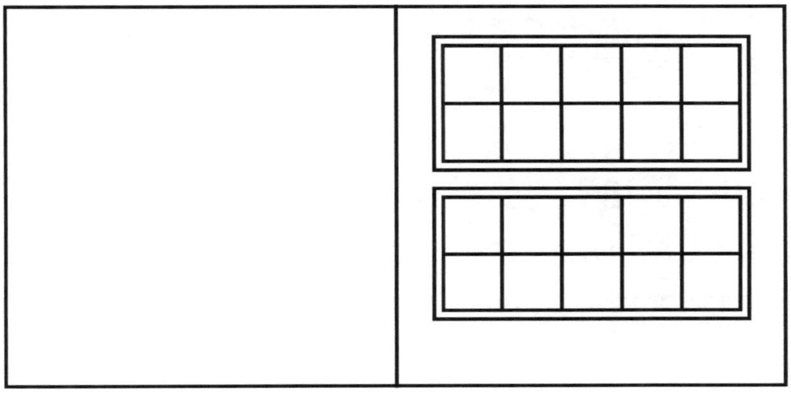

+	

Build these addition stories.
Record the answers on the charts.

7	4
+ 1	7

2	8
+ 2	3

3	9
+ 2	0

3	1
+ 1	9

Focus | Children use materials to build, find, and record sums of two-digit numbers using the standard algorithm.

Name: ______________________ Date: ______________________

Addition Stories

Build these addition stories on a place-value mat.
Record the answers on this page.

28 + 11	34 + 23	44 + 18	89 + 16
26 + 34	52 + 18	46 + 35	19 + 65

What other way can you solve 52 + 18?
Show your way using pictures, numbers, or words.

Choose an addition story you can solve a different way.
Show your way using pictures, numbers, or words.

Focus | Children find the sums using the standard algorithm. They choose different ways to find the sums of two-digit numbers.

HOME CONNECTION
Have your child describe at least two ways to solve 29 + 39, with and without materials.

Name: ____________________ Date: ____________________

Read All about It!

Leo has 65 comic books.
He gave 28 of them to Lizzie.
How many comic books does Leo have now?

Use materials. Solve the story problem.
Show how you solved it.

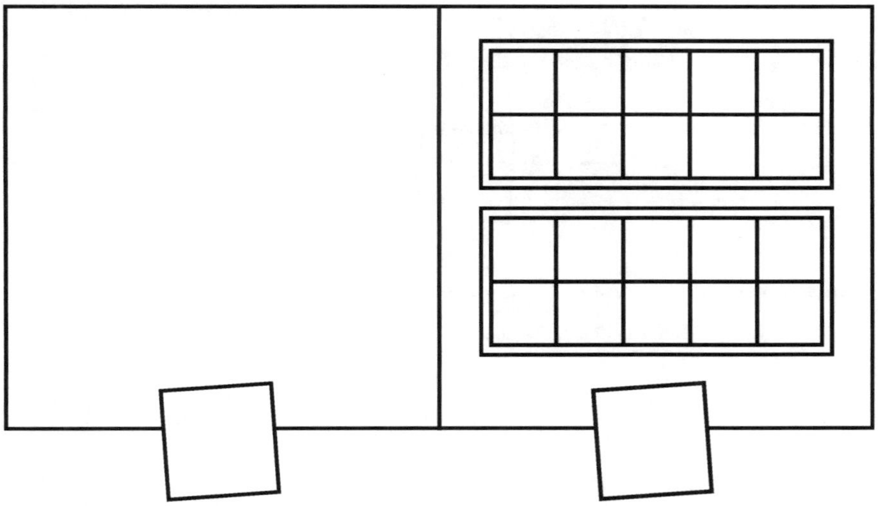

Can you think of another way to solve the problem?
Show it here.

Focus | Children use base ten concepts and materials to solve a subtraction problem.

Name: ____________________ Date: ____________________

Bookworm Bonanza

Leo and Lizzie joined a comic book club.
The book club has 96 comic books to share.
The first week, Lizzie borrowed 18 of them.
How many were left?

Use materials.
Solve the story problem.
Show how you solved it.

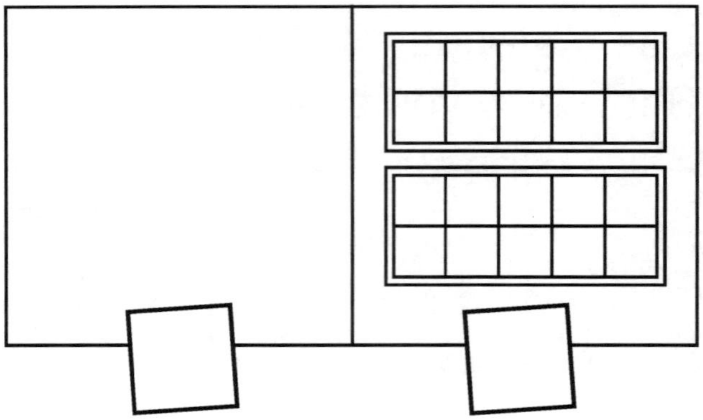

Another week, Leo brought in 24 comic books.
Lizzie brought in 17.
Who brought in more?
How many more?

Solve the story problem.
Show how you solved it.

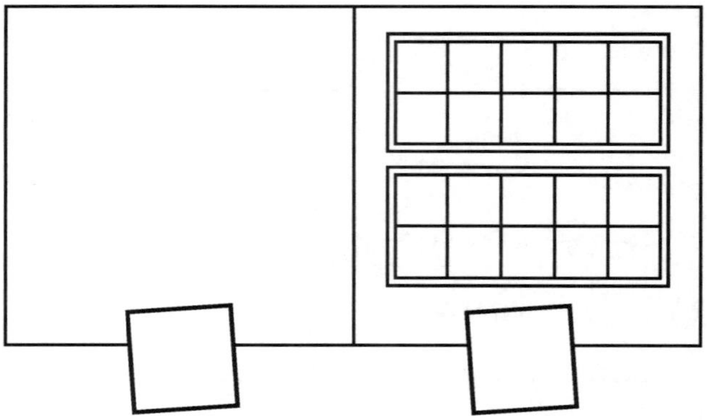

Make your own story problem. Solve it.

Focus | Children create and solve story problems using place-value concepts.

Name: ______________________ Date: ______________________

The Bookworm List

Make a story problem about the book list.
Solve your problem.
Show your work in pictures, words, or numbers.

Make another story problem.
Change books with a partner.
Solve your partner's problem.

Partner's Name

____

Focus | Children create and solve story problems using place-value concepts. Then they solve a partner's problem.

Name: ______________________ Date: ______________________

What's the Difference?

Which subtraction stories do you think will need a trade? Circle them.

Use a place-value mat to solve the questions you circled.

69 – 39 = _____	53 – 14 = _____	65 – 26 = _____
33 – 18 = _____	64 – 57 = _____	93 – 30 = _____

Write the problems that do not need a trade. Solve them.

FOCUS Children identify the subtraction sentences that require trading, and use materials to find the answers. For the remaining subtraction sentences, children find the answers in their own way.

HOME CONNECTION Have your child tell about one number sentence that required trading. Ask your child: "How did the place-value mat help you find the answer?"

Name: ______________________ Date: ______________________

How Many Fossils?

Dr. Rockhound's 53 fossils
are made up of shells and rocks.
Naveen counted 27 shells.
How many rocks does Dr. Rockhound have?

Build the subtraction story on a place-value mat.
Record it here.
Then record the subtraction using numbers.

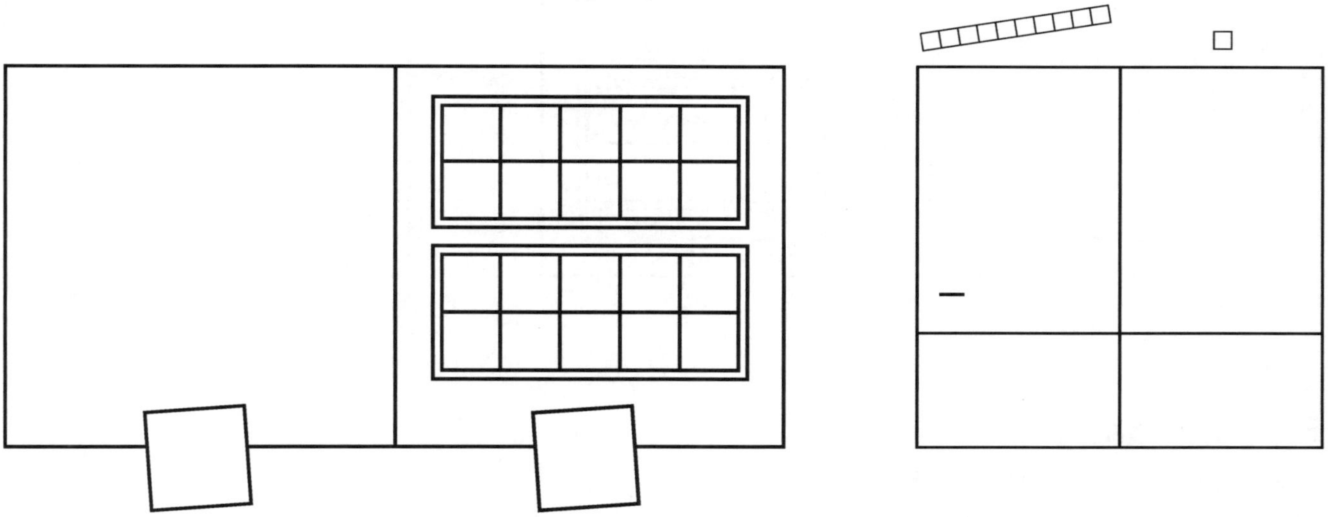

How are your picture and your
number recording alike?

____

How are they different?

____

FOCUS | Children use materials to solve a subtraction problem using the standard algorithm, and record their work.

Name: ____________________ Date: ____________________

At the Museum

There are 75 children at the museum.
36 children visit the fossils.
The others visit the cave exhibit.
How many children are at the cave exhibit?

Build the subtraction story on a place-value mat.
Record it here.
Then record the subtraction using numbers.

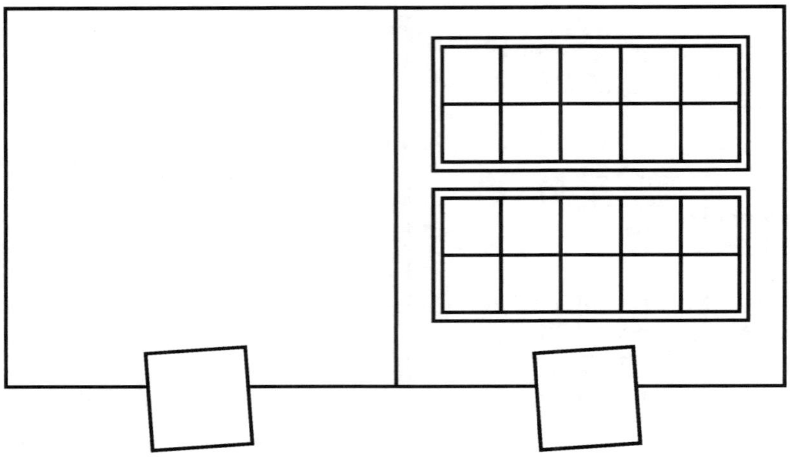

Tens	Ones
–	

Find the answers.
Use your base 10 materials for each.

Tens	Ones
7	8
– 4	5

Tens	Ones
3	2
– 1	3

Tens	Ones
5	5
– 2	8

Tens	Ones
6	7
– 2	8

Focus | Children use materials to build, find, and record differences of two-digit numbers using the standard algorithm.

Name: ______________________ Date: ______________________

Subtraction Stories

Build these subtraction stories.
Use Snap Cubes and a place-value mat.
Record the answers on this page.

5	2
− 3	5

8	7
− 3	7

6	5
− 3	8

8	6
− 5	9

1	7
−	9

7	0
− 1	9

8	9
− 1	8

8	0
− 7	5

Show another way to find 70 – 19. Use pictures, numbers, or words.

Choose a subtraction story you can solve a different way.
Show it using pictures, numbers, or words.

Focus Children use materials to build subtraction stories using the standard algorithm. They then solve subtraction stories in different ways.

HOME CONNECTION Have your child describe two ways to solve 80 – 75, with and without materials.

Name: ______________________ Date: ______________________

What's in Pat's Pockets?

Pat has 4 coins in her pocket.
What could the coins be?
How much money might Pat have?

Show how you solved the problem.
Use pictures, numbers, or words.

Focus | Children choose 4 coins and find their combined value.

Name: ______________________ Date: ______________________

Name the Coins

There is 83¢ in Joe's piggy bank.
He empties his bank and counts the coins.
What could the coins be?

Show how to solve the problem.
Use pictures, numbers, or words.

Focus | Children choose a strategy to solve a problem.

HOME CONNECTION

Take turns with your child creating money riddles. Model a money amount without showing it, then give the total and the number of coins.

Name: ______________________ Date: ______________________

At the Book Fair

Jenn unpacked the 55 nature books.
She unpacked the 28 puzzle books.
How many books did Jenn unpack altogether?

Use materials. Show your answer.

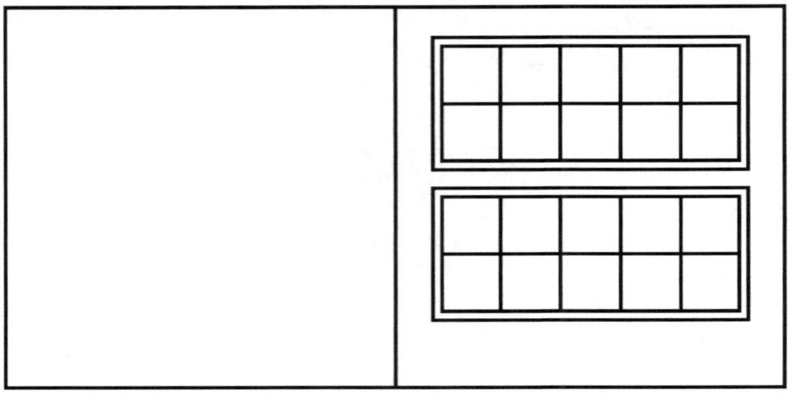

Rae put price stickers on all 78 picture books.
Jenn put price stickers on all 28 puzzle books.
How many more books did Rae stick with stickers?

Use materials. Show your answer.

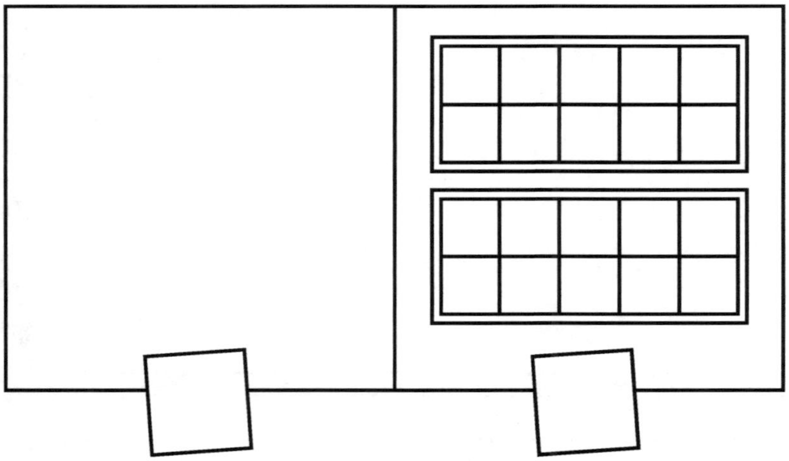

Focus | Children solve story problems involving addition and subtraction, using place-value concepts by modelling on a place-value chart. They record solutions pictorially.

Name: ______________________ Date: ______________________

Books on Order

	Monday	Tuesday	Wednesday
number of books ordered	26	43	79

Make an addition story about the books ordered.
Show your addition story on a place-value mat.
Record the addition using numbers.

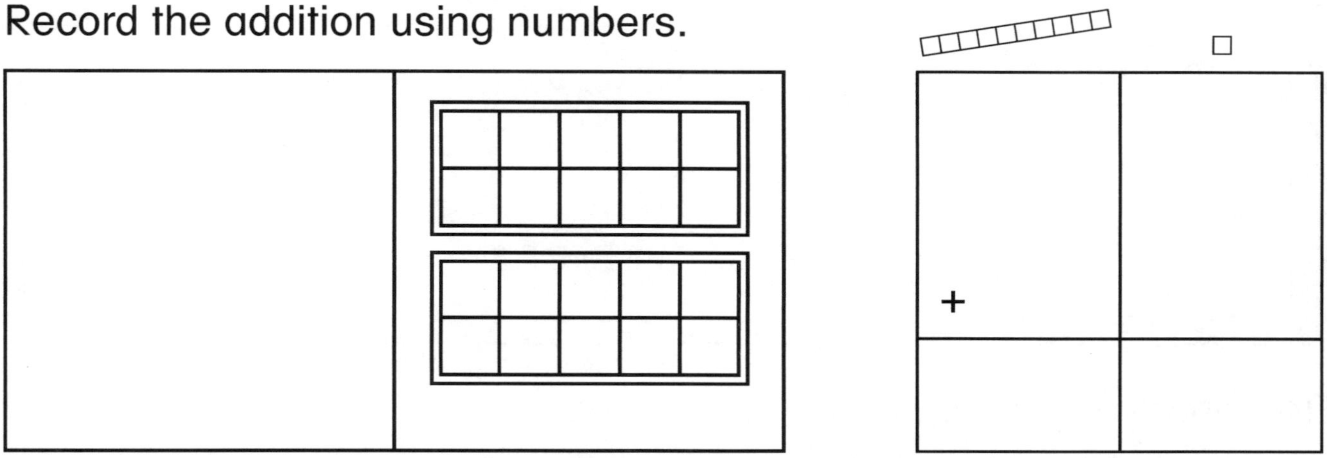

Make a subtraction story about the books ordered.
Show your subtraction story on a place-value mat.
Record the subtraction using numbers.

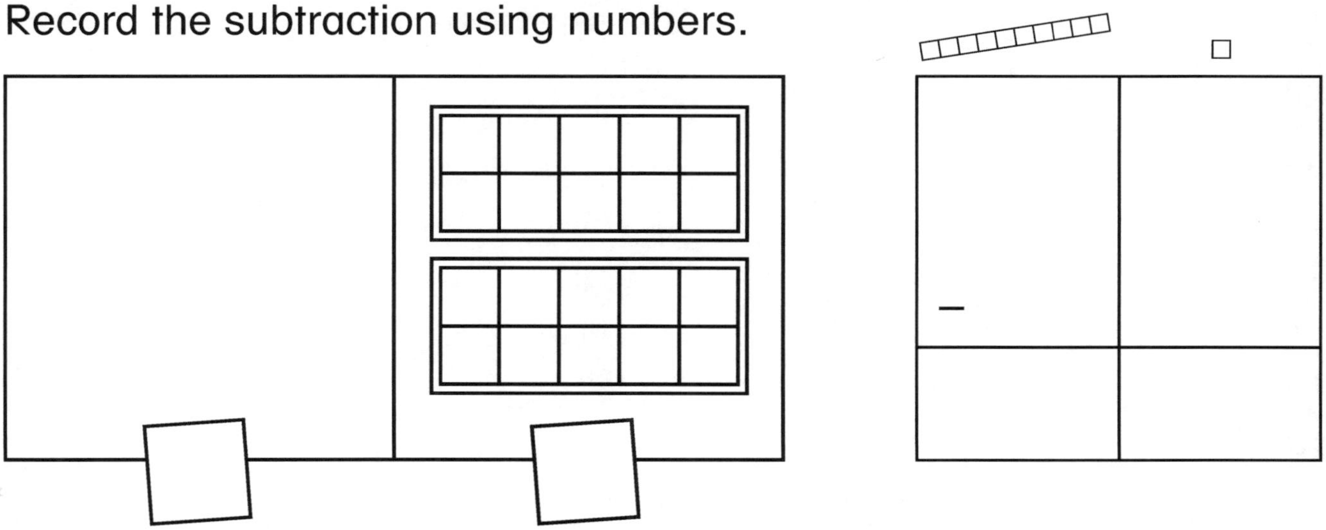

Focus | Children create and solve story problems related to addition and subtraction of two-digit numbers. They record solutions pictorially and symbolically.

Name: ______________________________ Date: ______________________________

My Journal

Tell what you learned about adding.
Use pictures, numbers, or words.

Tell what you learned about subtracting.
Use pictures, numbers, or words.

Focus | Children reflect on and record what they learned about adding and subtracting using the standard algorithm.

Planning "Spring Fling"

Cam ran through the door. "I'm home!" he called out.
The dog came to see what the noise was about.
"We're having a 'Spring Fling'—a school celebration.
I've brought you your own special 'Fling' invitation!"

Take-Home Story

The next day Grade 2 started planning and thinking.
"What snacks will we serve? What will people be drinking?
How will we decorate? Where will we sit?"
Grandma thought, "Maybe I'll help out a bit."

Miss Chu said, "We'll greet people when they arrive.
If everyone comes, there will be 75!
We'll hand out the programs we make at the door.
We'll keep extras here in this box on the floor."

“We’ll need a large space that can fit us all in.
We can hang up spring posters to show in the gym!
How will we set up the tables and chairs?
I hope there’s enough. I hope we have spares!”

They brainstormed together for more than an hour.
"We should practise a song for the Primary choir.
Reciting a spring poem would be special, too.
Are there any more things the Grade 2 class might do?"

They posted a graph that they studied a lot.
Cam asked, "Is there anything that we forgot?"
They grew more excited as every day passed.
Then finally the day came. They all sighed, "At last!"

They'd planned very well. They were all well prepared.
But they ran out of programs, so everyone shared.
The families grew quiet. The choir came in.
"Welcome," Cam said. "Let the 'Spring Fling' begin!"

About the Story

The story was read in class to prepare for a Mathematics Investigation activity. Children asked questions about and made predictions from a bar graph. They added and subtracted two-digit numbers, recognized a growing pattern, and counted by 10s.

Talk about It Together

- Have you ever planned an event like "Spring Fling" before? What are the kinds of things you had to think about? How did knowing math help you?
- Is there anything you would have done differently than the Grade 2 class?
- How were the students feeling as they planned the event?
- What is your favourite part of the story?

At the Library

Ask your local librarian about other good books to share about numbers, collecting and analyzing information, and geometric shapes.

What Will We Do?

Look at the graph.
Write 3 things you can learn from the graph.

1. ______________________________

2. ______________________________

3. ______________________________

The Grade 1 class made a graph about what they would like to do for the "Spring Fling."

Would the graph be the same or different than the Grade 2 graph?

In what ways would the graph be the same or different?
Use pictures, numbers, or words to explain your thinking.

Think of something different the Grade 2 class could make a graph about to help them in their planning.

____

How Many Are Coming?

All the primary classes invited their families.
Some moms and dads are coming.
Some grandparents and friends are coming, too.

Look at the tally chart.
Count the tally marks for each class.
Write the number of guests in the last column.

Class	Tally of Guests	How Many Are Coming?
Kindergarten	卌 卌 卌 卌 卌	_______ guests
Grade 1	卌 卌 卌	_______ guests
Grade 2	卌 卌 卌 卌 卌 卌 卌	_______ guests

How many guests are coming altogether? ________
Show how you solved the problem.

Show two ways to arrange the guests' chairs in groups.

I made my groups this way because ____________________

____.

I made my groups this way because ____________________

____.

Write a subtraction problem about the guests and show how to solve it.

How Many Cans?

The school is having a food drive.
Families bring 92 cans of food.
The children stack the cans in pyramids of 10s.

How many pyramids of 10s can they build? _______

How many cans will be left over? _______
Show your thinking in pictures, numbers, or words.

Describe the pattern you see in the pyramid.

____

Suppose the children add another row to one pyramid.

How many cans of food would be in this new row? _______

How many cans of food would be in the new pyramid? _______

Suppose the children continue to add rows to one pyramid.

How many rows would the largest pyramid have? _______
Show your thinking in pictures, numbers, or words.

Crazy Container Tally

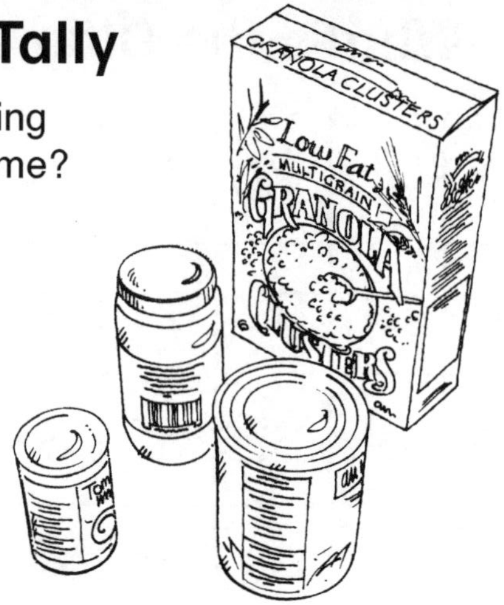

Which types of food packaging are most popular in your home?

Cans? Boxes? Jars? Plastic containers?

Get ready to investigate by printing each category on a piece of paper.

The search is on! Tally each one you find.

When you are done, use all the information to create a "Food Package" bar graph.

Tell someone about what you found. Which was most popular? Least popular? Were you surprised?

Name the Missing Buttons

Seven buttons are in a bag.

One button was taken out and then put back in. Here are eight draws.

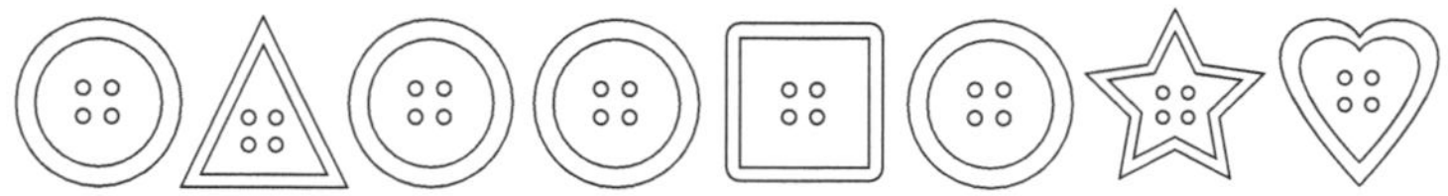

What shapes do you think the last two buttons were?

 The next 4 pages fold in half to make an 8-page booklet.

Fold

Math at Home

Math at Home 2

Mystery Solids

Game

Put 5 or 6 small 3-D solids
into a bag you cannot see through.
Reach in and take 1 of the solids.
Challenge a friend to guess
your solid by asking yes
or no questions.
Only 10 questions are allowed.

If your friend guesses
the solid, show it.
Then give the bag to your
friend and play again.
You guess this time!

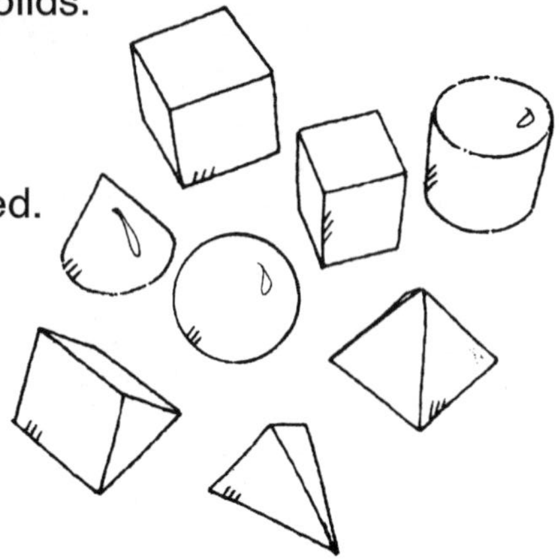

Adding Stars

How many stars altogether?

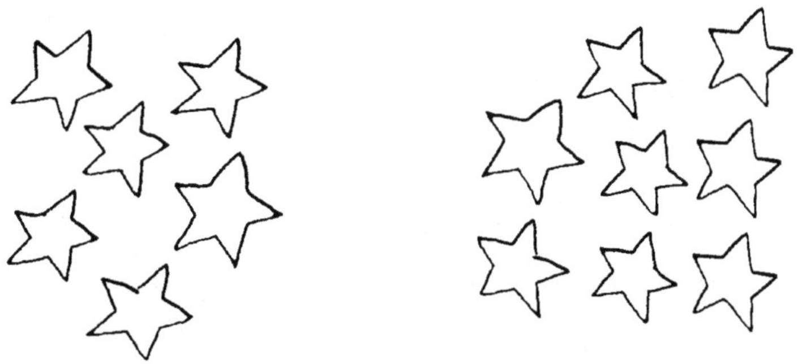

Sean said, "8 and 2 more is 10. And 4 more is 14."

Amy said, "I know 8 and 8 is 16.
If I take 2 away, it's 14."

Who's right? Why do you think so?

What's the Difference? Game Board

10	11	12	13	14	15	16	17	18	19
20	21	22	23	24	25	26	27	28	29
30	31	32	33	34	35	36	37	38	39
40	41	42	43	44	45	46	47	48	49
50	51	52	53	54	55	56	57	58	59
60	61	62	63	64	65	66	67	68	69
70	71	72	73	74	75	76	77	78	79
80	81	82	83	84	85	86	87	88	89
90	91	92	93	94	95	96	97	98	99

What's the Difference?

Game

You'll need:
- game board (page 7)
- two sets of number cards, 1 to 9 and one 0 card, in a bag you cannot see through
- 6 counters
- paper
- pencil

On your turn:
- Draw 2 cards and use them to make a two-digit number. Put a counter on the matching number on the game board.
- Draw 2 more cards and make another two-digit number. Use a counter to cover this number on the game board.
- Find the difference between the 2 numbers by counting how many 10s and 1s they are away from each other. Use a counter to cover this number.

If the numbers **33** and **57** were covered, you would say, "57 is two 10s and four 1s away from 33. The difference is 24."

If the difference is

- more than 25, you get a point.
- a number with a ☆ you get a point.
- a number with a ♡ your friend gets a point.

After tallying the points, place the cards back in the bag and remove your counters from the board.

Take turns until someone gets 10 points.

At the Fair

Game

How many different ways could you win this carnival game?

Snack Time

You want to buy an apple and you have this much money.

Do you have enough?

If not, how much more do you need?

Out at the Park

Next time you are at the park, look around at the play equipment. What shapes do you see? Do you notice any patterns?

Four in a Row

Game

You'll need:
- addition chart (page 5)
- number cards 1 to 9
- two kinds of small counters (beans, buttons)

Put the addition chart and cards between both players. Cards should be face down.

Each player gets a pile of counters.

On your turn:
- Draw 2 cards and say 2 addition sentences that match the numbers.
- Put one of your counters on either of the matching sums on the chart.
  So, if you drew **8** and **6**, you would put your counter on the sum of 8 + 6 or 6 + 8.
- Put the cards back down and move them around.

Take turns until someone gets 4 counters in a row.
Remember to try to block the other player!

What patterns do you see?

Addition Chart for Four in a Row

+	0	1	2	3	4	5	6	7	8	9
0	0	1	2	3	4	5	6	7	8	9
1	1	2	3	4	5	6	7	8	9	10
2	2	3	4	5	6	7	8	9	10	11
3	3	4	5	6	7	8	9	10	11	12
4	4	5	6	7	8	9	10	11	12	13
5	5	6	7	8	9	10	11	12	13	14
6	6	7	8	9	10	11	12	13	14	15
7	7	8	9	10	11	12	13	14	15	16
8	8	9	10	11	12	13	14	15	16	17
9	9	10	11	12	13	14	15	16	17	18

UNIT 8

Linear Measurement, Area, and Perimeter

Focus | Children look for ways people are measuring to prepare classroom decorations.

Name: ______________________________ Date: ______________________________

Dear Family,

In this unit, your child will be learning about measurement. Your child will develop an understanding of linear measurement and area.

The Learning Goals for this unit are to

- Estimate, measure, and compare lengths using non-standard units, such as paper clips, straws, or Snap Cube trains.
- Develop an understanding of the need for standard units and measure lengths using the centimetre and the metre.
- Estimate, measure, and compare perimeter (distance around) using non-standard and standard units.
- Investigate area measurement by using non-standard units, such as cards, to cover a surface.
- Solve everyday problems about measurement.

You can help your child achieve these goals by doing the Home Connection activities suggested at the bottom of selected pages.

Name: ______________________ Date: ______________________

My Banner Measurements

Draw your desk. Where will you put your banner?
Tell how you measured it.
Use pictures, numbers, or words.

Focus | Children draw their desk and a banner to decorate it. Then, they tell how they measured the desk to prepare for the decoration activity.

Name: ______________________ Date: ______________________

Measure Three Ways

Choose two objects to measure.

I chose ____________________ and ____________________.

Measure each object 3 times, using 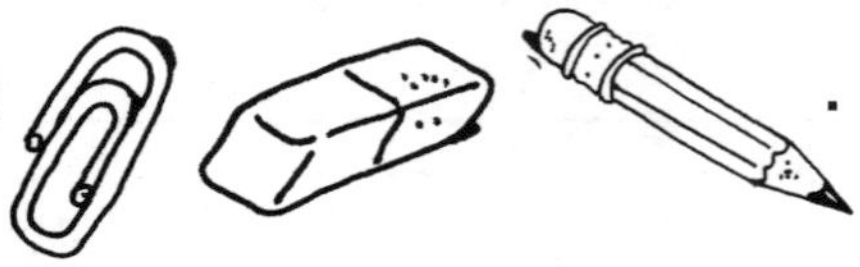.
Estimate before each measure.
Complete each table.

My first object is ____________________.

Measuring Unit	Estimate	Measure
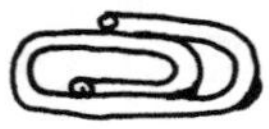		

My second object is ____________________.

Measuring Unit	Estimate	Measure
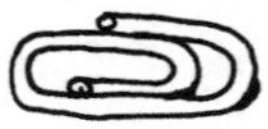		

Compare your measurements. What do you notice?

____

____

Focus | Children estimate and measure the lengths of two objects using a variety of non-standard units and compare results.

Name: ______________________ Date: ______________________

Estimate, Measure, and Compare

Choose four books.
What will you use to measure their heights?
Circle one. 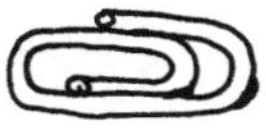  

Complete the table.

Book Title	Height

Put the books on the shelf in order of their heights.
What other ways can you order the books?

____

____

____

What other ways can you measure the books?

____

____

____

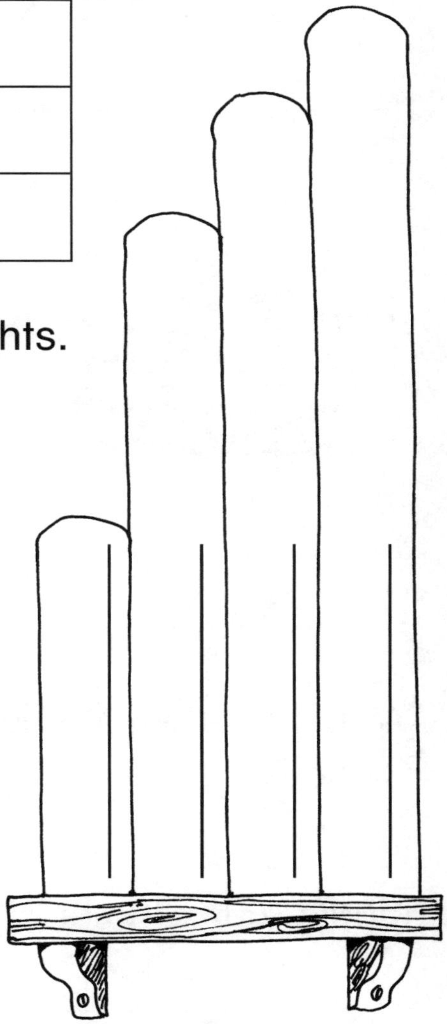

HOME CONNECTION

Choose something in your home that you and your child can order together by length (for example, clothes in a closet, towels on a rod).

Focus | Children measure and compare the heights of four books.

Name: ______________________ Date: ______________________

Real-Life Beetles

The pictures match the size of each beetle in real life.
About how long is each one?

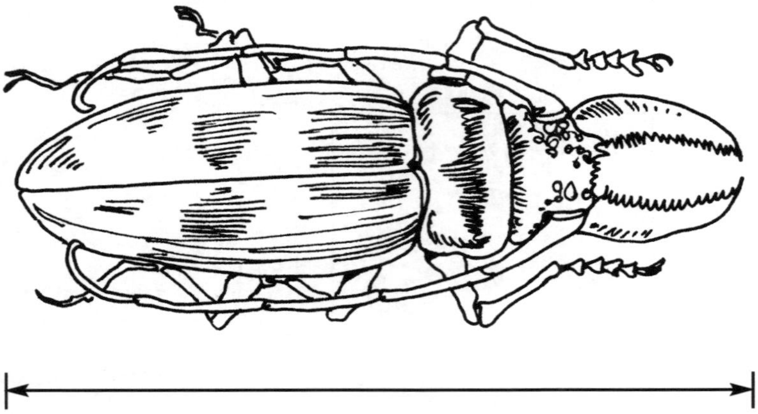

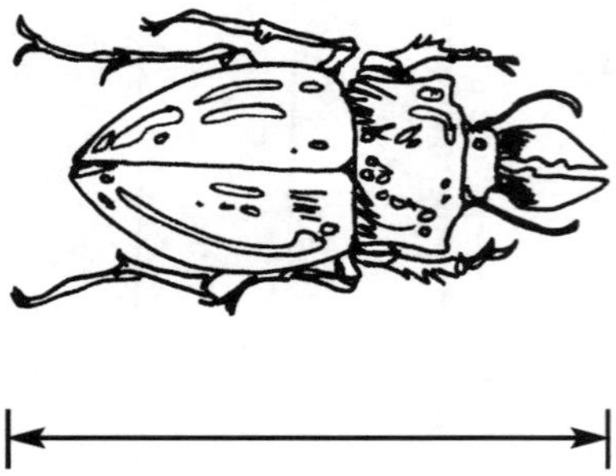

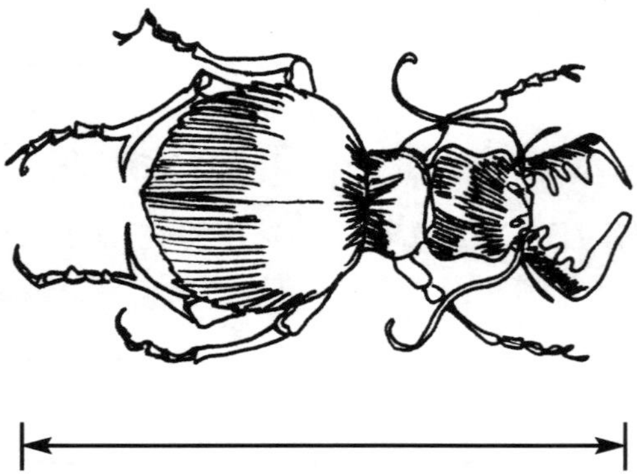

Which beetle is the longest?
Circle it.

Which beetle do you think is the widest?
Measure to check. Were you right?

____

____

Focus | Children measure and compare the lengths of spiders using a centimetre ruler.

Name: ______________________________ Date: ______________________________

Calling all 10s

Find four objects that you think are each about 10 cm long.

Measure them and write their lengths.

Object	Length
	______________ cm
	______________ cm
	______________ cm
	______________ cm

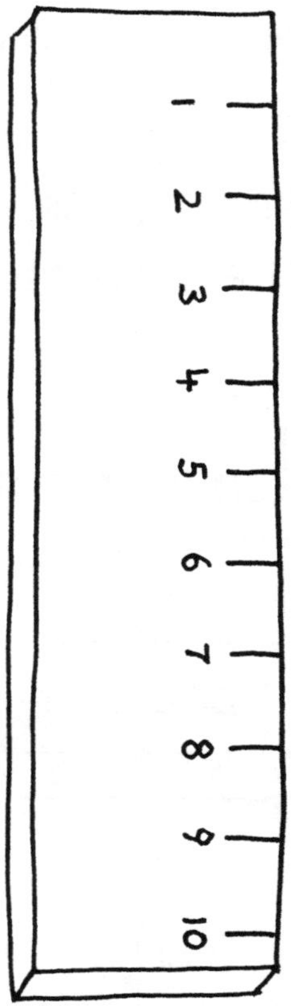

What helped you to find objects about 10 cm long?

____

____

HOME CONNECTION

With your child, find three things in the kitchen that are about 10 cm long. Ask your child to measure with a centimetre ruler to check.

Focus | Children estimate and then use a ruler to measure four objects, each about 10 cm long.

Name: ______________________ Date: ______________________

About How Long Is a Metre?

Choose three objects in the classroom.
Look for

- one object that is shorter than 1 m long
- one object that is longer than 1 m long
- one object that is about 1 m long

Complete the table.
Name each object and estimate its length.
Then, measure it.

	My Object	**Estimate**	**Measure**
shorter than 1 m			
longer than 1 m			
about 1 m			

Focus | Children choose objects that are longer than, shorter than, and about, 1 m long. They estimate and measure the length of each object.

Name: ______________________ Date: ______________________

Which Unit?

What would you use to measure these objects?
Circle centimetre or metre.

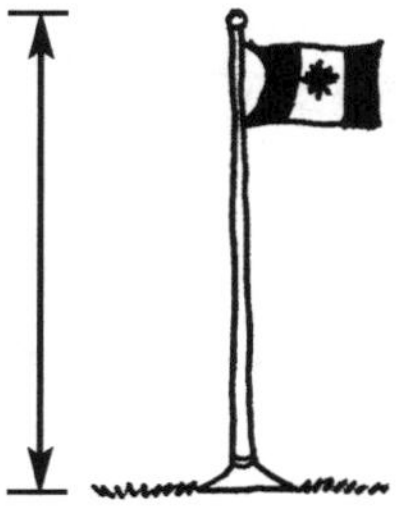

centimetre metre

centimetre metre

centimetre metre

centimetre metre

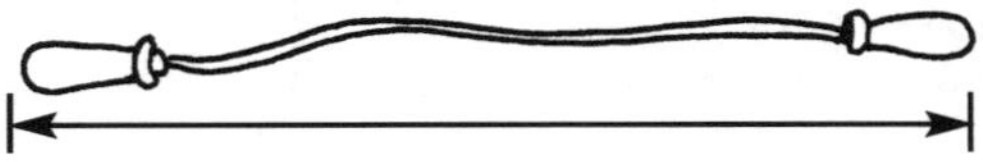

centimetre metre

Choose one of your answers. Tell about your thinking.

____

____

HOME CONNECTION

Have your child estimate and measure the heights of family members using metres, centimetres, or both.

Focus | Children decide whether they would use the centimetre or the metre to measure each of the pictured objects.

Name: ____________________ Date: ____________________

Poster Space

Measure the wall spaces in your classroom.

Record each measure in the table.

Wall Space	Width
1	
2	
3	

Put the widths in order from least to greatest.

__________ __________ __________

HOME CONNECTION

With your child, look for items that can be ordered by length (for example, winter scarves, belts, ties). Place the objects in order of length to show the comparison.

Focus | Children order the widths of specified wall spaces in their classroom to determine which one will best fit a poster.

Name: ______________________ Date: ______________________

Measure and Graph

Find 4 objects to measure.

books magazines

shoes

your choice

pencil cases

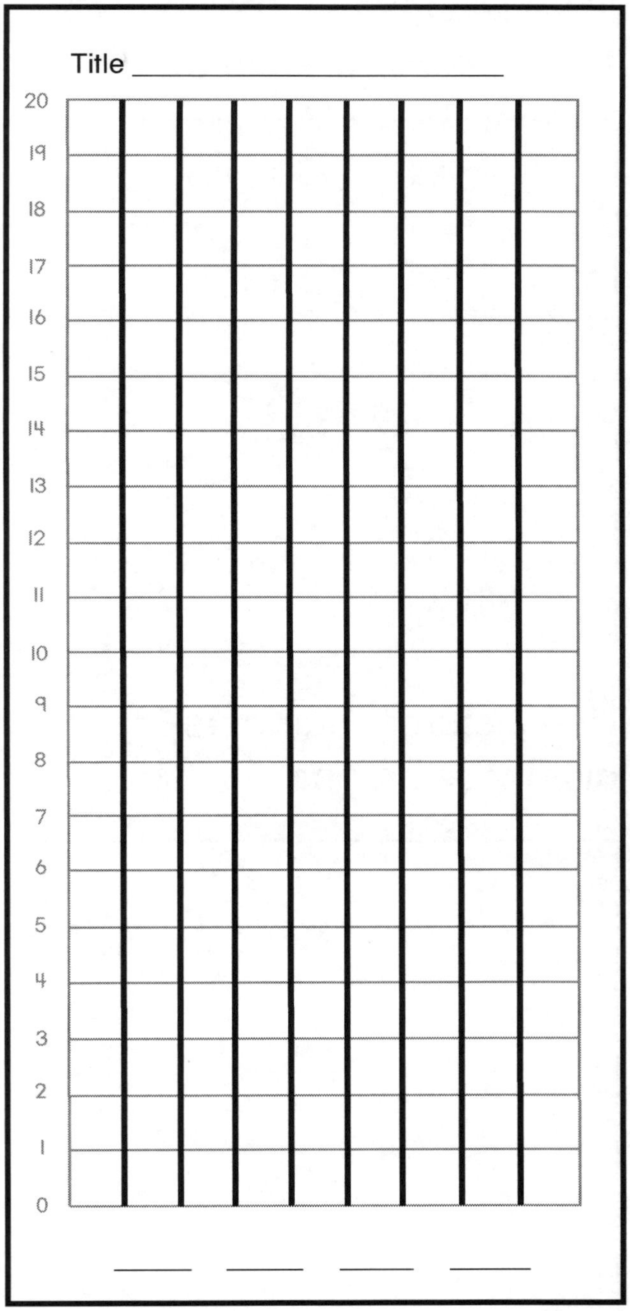

Complete the table.

My Objects	Measure
	______ cm
	______ cm
	______ cm
	______ cm

Make a graph to show your measurements.

Write your measurements from shortest to longest.

__________ __________ __________ __________

Focus | Children measure 4 objects, then graph and order their results.

Name: ______________________ Date: ______________________

Distance Around

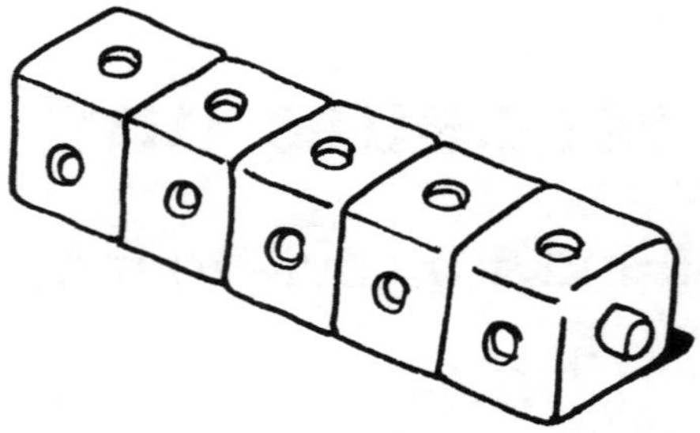

Draw pictures of the figures you measured.
Inside each figure, write the distance around.

Use pictures, numbers, or words to tell how you found the distances around.

Focus | Children find the perimeter of several large figures on the classroom floor.

HOME CONNECTION

Choose a photograph with your child and have your child find the distance around it. Then, measure and cut paper to make a decorative frame.

Name: ______________________ Date: ______________________

Frame It

Find the distance around each picture.
Measure 3 times.

distance around ________ cm

distance around ________ cm

distance around ________ cm

Which picture has the shortest distance around? Circle it.

Focus | Children measure distances around pictures.

Name: ______________________ Date: ______________________

Cover It

You need to tile the dollhouse floor.
Choose one figure to cover the floor.
This is your unit. Circle it.

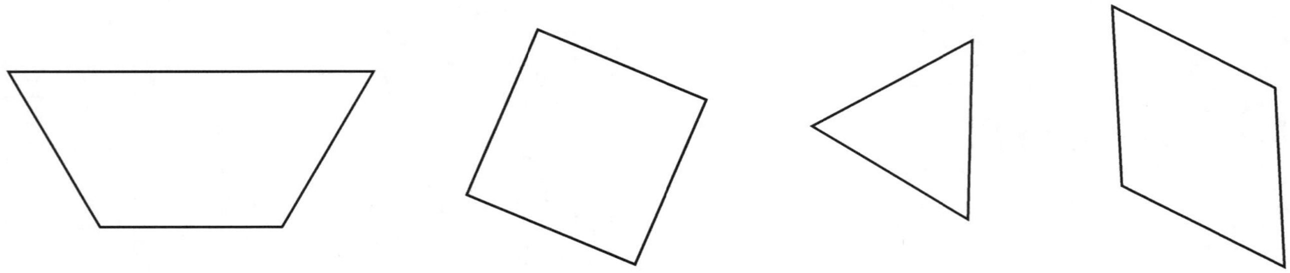

How many units do you think you will need? __________
Cover the floor.
How many units did you need? __________

Focus | Children select a non-standard unit to tile a rectangular area. They determine the number of units they need.

Name: ______________________ Date: ______________________

About How Many?

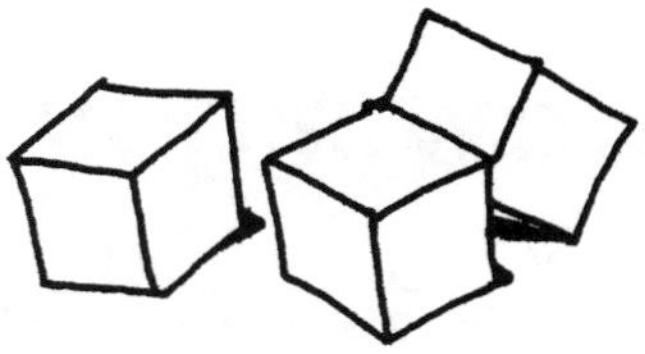

About how many blocks will cover each surface?

Object	Estimate	Measure
 the top of your desk	about ______	
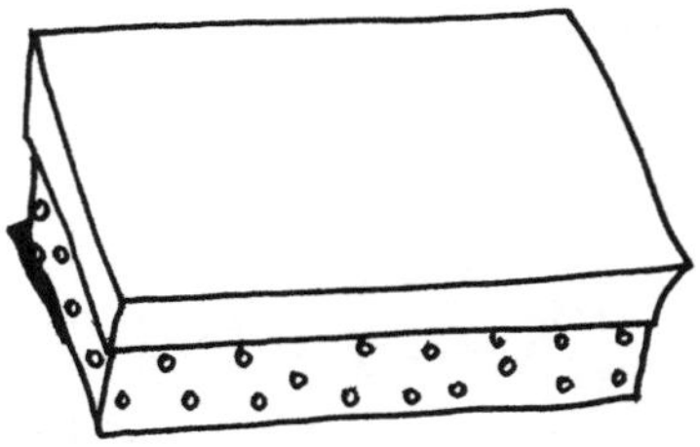 a box lid	about ______	
my object	about ______	

Suppose you measured again with another unit.
What do you think would happen?

____

____

FOCUS Children use materials to measure the area of surfaces in the classroom.

HOME CONNECTION Have your child find the area of a tabletop or counter using index cards. Use the measurement to create a paper cover for the table or to make placemats.

Name: ______________________ Date: ______________________

How Many Ways?

Make different arrangements
with 5 Snap Cubes.
How many arrangements can you find?
Show all your arrangements.

Focus | Children make different arrangements with 5 Snap Cubes and record them on grid paper.

Name: ______________________ Date: ______________________

Triangle Figures

Make different arrangements with 5 Pattern Block triangles.
Record your arrangements.

HOME CONNECTION

Use a word game that has letter tiles, and with your child, create the names of family members. For each name, look for different ways to arrange the number of tiles used.

FOCUS | Children make different arrangements with 5 Pattern Block triangles and record them on grid paper.

Name: ______________________________ Date: ______________________________

Our Obstacle Course

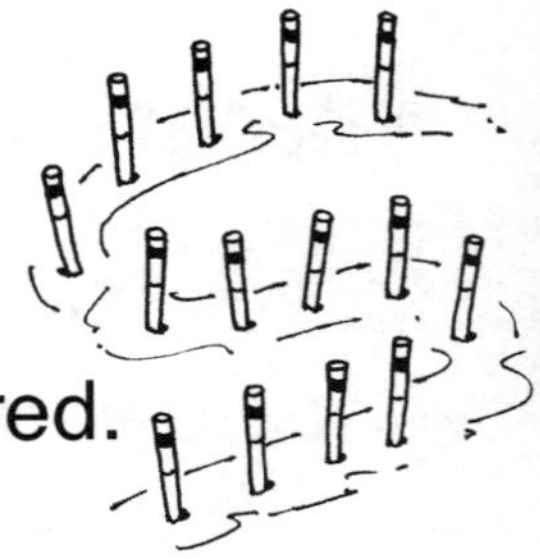

Measure the distance around your course in 2 ways.
Use pictures, numbers, or words to show how you measured.

First way

What is the distance around? ______________________________

Second way

What is the distance around? ______________________________

Measure the area your course covers. Use any way you like.
Show what you did in pictures, numbers, or words.

How we measured the course

How big is the course? ______________________________

Focus | Children measure distance around and the area of an obstacle course. They choose their own measuring units and instruments.

Name: ______________________ Date: ______________________

Making the Obstacle Course

Estimate how long the course is altogether.

____

Measure to find out. ____________________

What part did you make more than I m long? ____________________

How long is it? ______________

What part is more than 5 cm high? ____________________

How high is it? ________

What part is more than I0 cm wide? ____________________

How wide is it? ________

How far is it from the start to the first obstacle? ____________________

What is the tallest part to climb? ___________

How tall is it? __________

How do you know it is the tallest? ____________________

Focus | Children create and measure an obstacle course.

Name: ______________________ Date: ______________________

My Journal

Tell what you have learned about measuring lengths.

Tell what you have learned about covering surfaces.

HOME CONNECTION

Ask your child: "Why do you think learning about measurement is important?"

Focus | Children tell what they have learned about linear measurement, area, and perimeter.

UNIT 9

2-D Geometry

FOCUS | Children talk about the picture and identify the 2-D figures they recognize.

Name: ______________________ Date: ______________________

Dear Family,

In this unit, your child will be learning more about 2-D geometric figures and symmetry.

The Learning Goals for this unit are to

- Describe, sort, and compare 2-D figures according to the number of sides and number of vertices (corners).
- Recognize figures that have symmetry, or matching parts.
- Make patterns using materials and pictures of 2-D figures.
- Use positional language to describe movement and location: *slide to the left, turn, above, beside.*

You can help your child achieve these goals by doing the Home Connection activities suggested at the bottom of selected pages.

Name: ______________________ Date: ______________________

My Picture

Use □ ○ ▭ and △.

Make a picture.

Tell about the figures you used.

____

____

Focus | Children create pictures using 2-D figures and describe their work.

Name: ______________________________ Date: ______________________________

Where Am I?

Look in your classroom.
Find an example of each figure.
Tell where you saw each one.

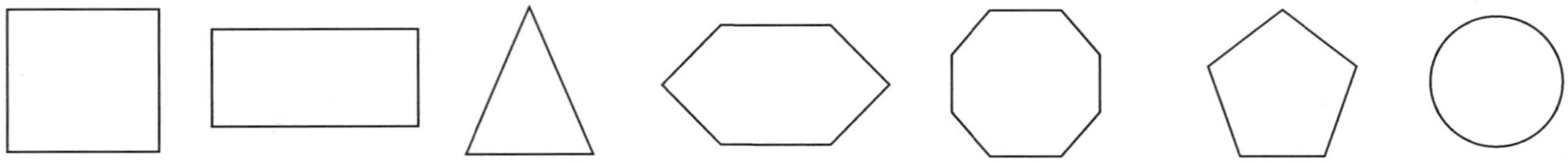

rectangle square triangle hexagon octagon pentagon circle

What I Saw	It Looks Like	Where I Saw It
book cover	a rectangle	inside my desk

Focus | Children look for geometric figures in the classroom and tell where each is located.

Name: ______________________________ Date: ______________________________

Look for It!

Colour a figure with 3 sides (red).

Colour a figure with 4 vertices (blue).

Colour a pentagon (green).

Colour a hexagon (purple).

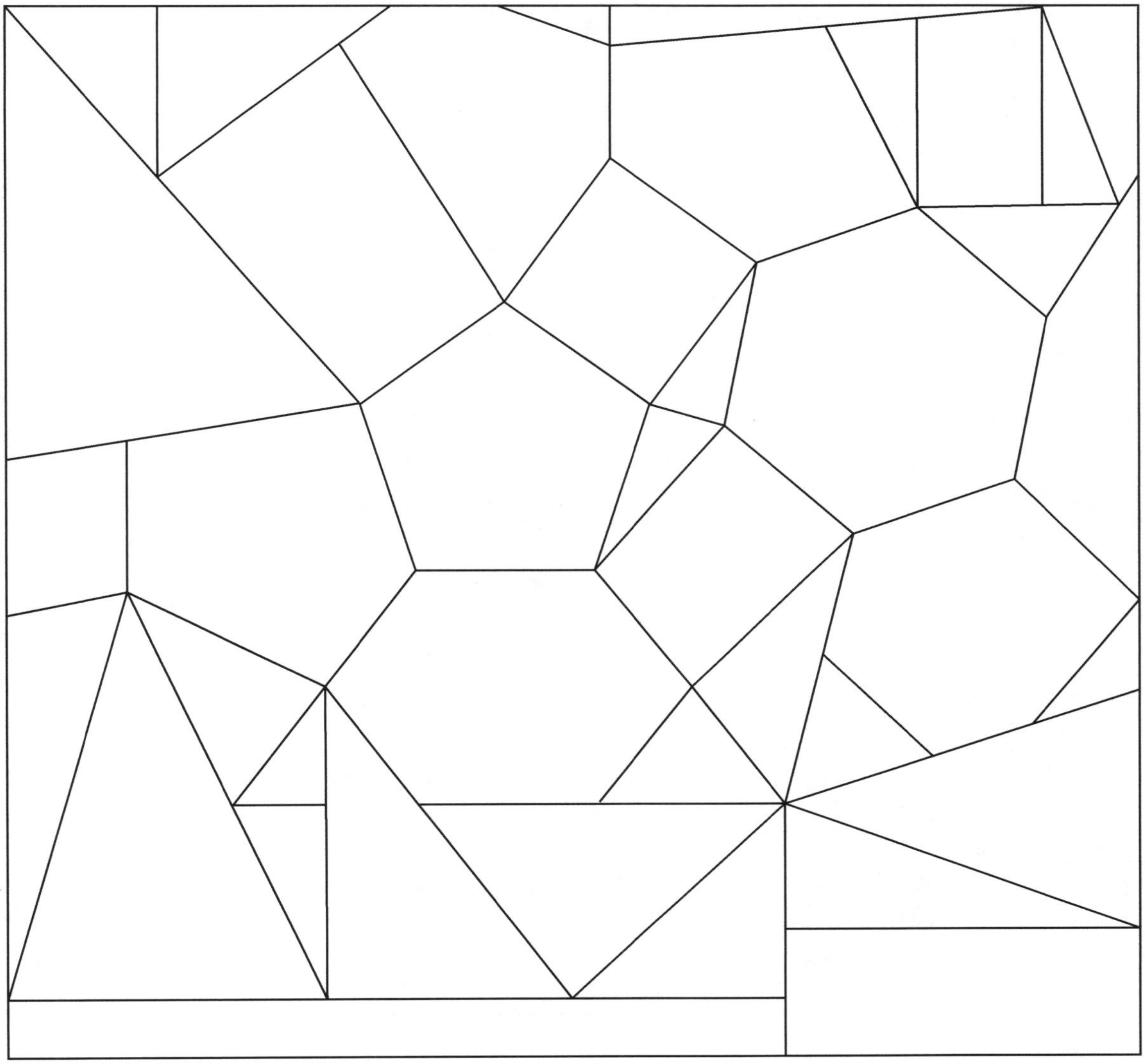

HOME CONNECTION

With your child, look for examples in your home of some of the figures your child has been learning about, such as circles, triangles, rectangles, pentagons, hexagons, and octagons. Which do you find most often?

Focus | Children look for and colour figures in a drawing.

Name: ______________________________ Date: ______________________________

Make a Match!

Choose a figure.
Find another child with a matching figure.

How do you know your figures match?
Use pictures, numbers, or words.

Focus | Children each choose a figure from a set and then look for a matching figure. They describe how they know that the figures match.

HOME CONNECTION

Cut out several pairs of matching triangles (same size and shape). Scramble them. Pick one triangle. Ask your child to find its match. After all are paired, ask: "What strategies did you use to match the triangles?"

Name: ______________________ Date: ______________________

Alike and Different

Circle 2 figures.

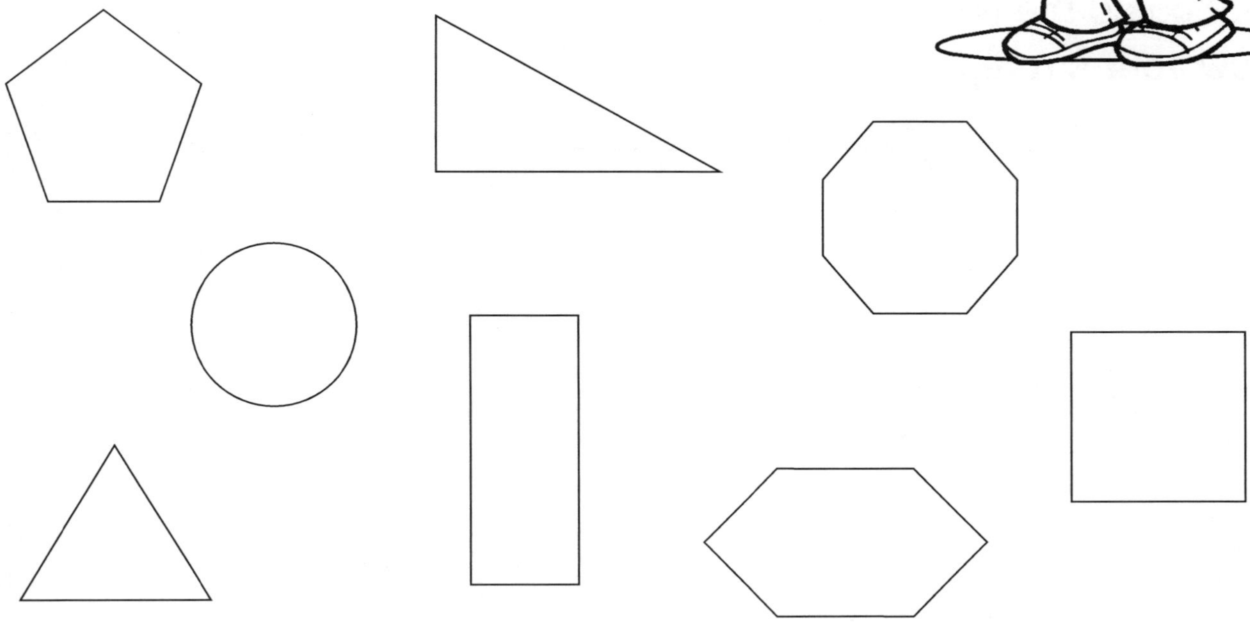

I chose the ________________ and the ____________________.

One way they are alike is ________________________________

____.

Another way they are alike is _____________________________

____.

One way they are different is _____________________________

____.

Focus | Children select 2 figures and describe how they are alike and different.

Name: ______________________________ Date: ______________________________

What Is in the Bag?

There are 3 figures in a bag.
The total number of sides is 13.

What could the figures be?
Show your strategy.

What other figures could they be?

Focus | Children choose a strategy to find 3 figures with a total number of 13 sides.

Name: ______________________ Date: ______________________

Another 3 in the Bag

There are 3 figures in a bag.
The total number of vertices is 12.

What could the figures be?
Show your strategy.

What other figures could they be?

Focus | Children choose a strategy to find 3 figures with a total number of 12 vertices.

HOME CONNECTION

With your child, go on a vertex (corner) hunt in your home. Look for a geometric figure and count its corners. Ask: "How can we find another figure with the same number of corners?"

Name: ______________________________ Date: ______________________________

Matching Parts

Circle the figures that have matching parts.
Draw the fold lines.

Focus | Children find matching parts on figures cut from *LM 3: Geometric Figures*. Then they circle the figures above that match those figures, and draw the fold lines.

Name: ______________________ Date: ______________________

Symmetry Cutouts

Fold a piece of paper in half.
Draw an outline for half a figure.
Begin on the fold line.
End on the fold line.

Keep your paper folded.
Cut on the outline. But do not cut on the fold line!
Open the paper and paste the figure below.

What happened when you opened up the paper?

____

Focus | Children create a symmetrical figure by folding paper and cutting. Then they answer a related question.

Name: ______________________ Date: ______________________

Draw Matching Parts

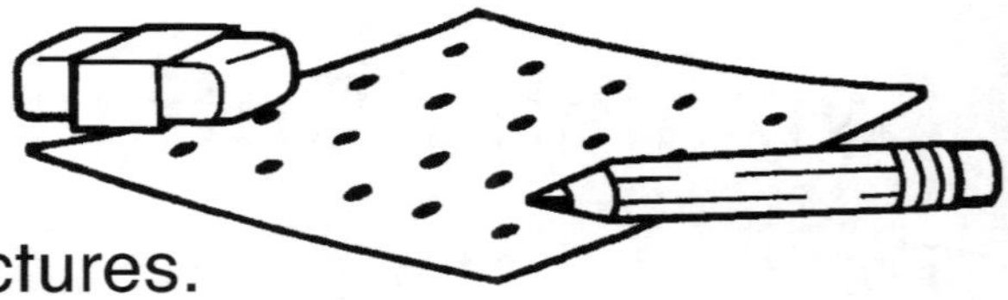

Draw the matching parts to finish the pictures.

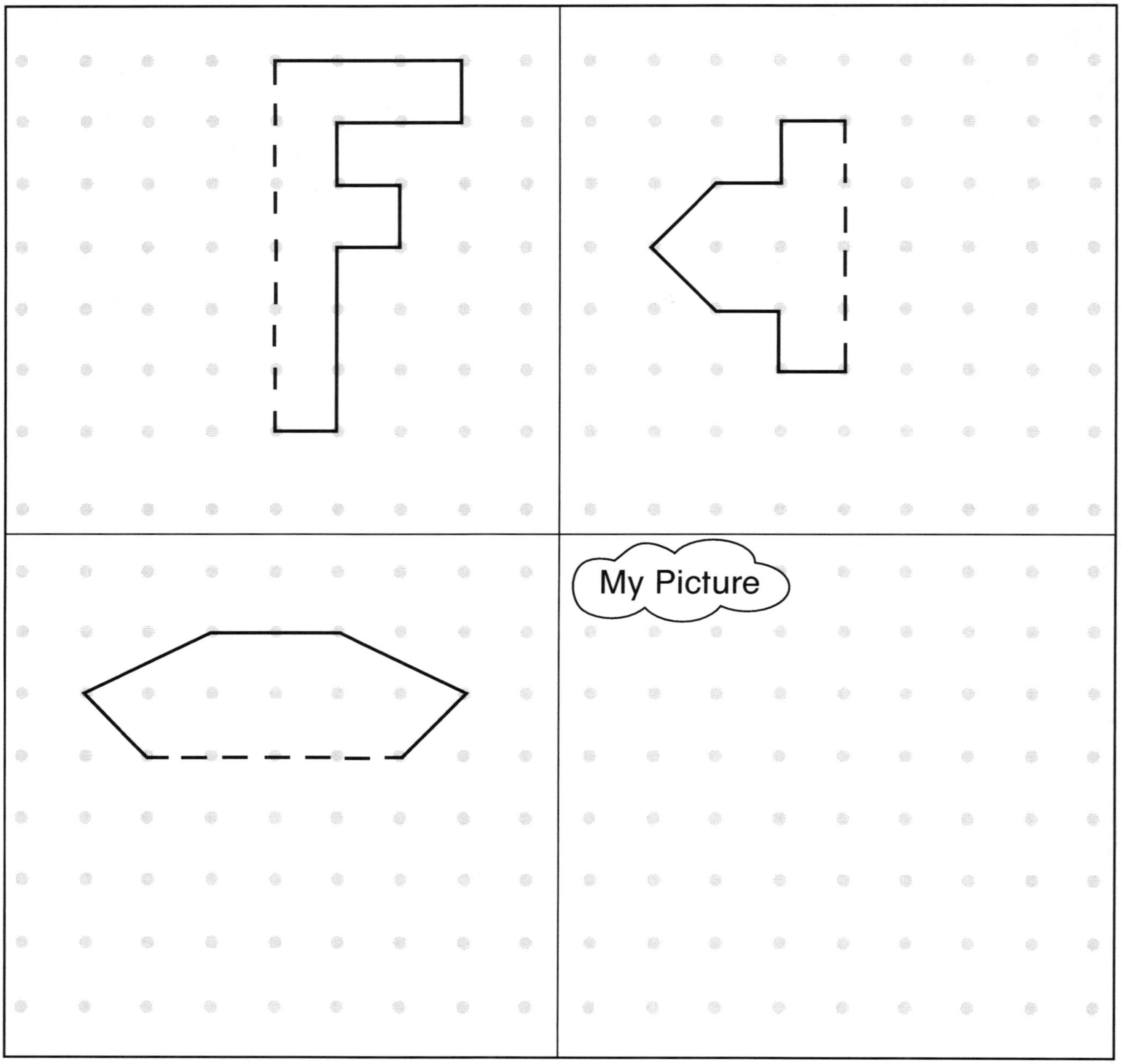

HOME CONNECTION

Create 3 to 6 symmetrical figures by folding paper in half and cutting. Cut each figure in half along the fold line. Mix the pieces and pick one. Ask your child to find its matching part. Have your child pair the rest of the pieces.

Focus | Children draw a "mirror image" to complete each symmetrical figure.

Name: ____________________ Date: ____________________

We Found Symmetry!

Put a Mira on the square.
Look for matching parts.

Use 

.
Draw a line where you put the Mira.

Look for another way.

Use 

.
Draw a line where you put the Mira.

How many ways can you find? ____________________

What did you find out?

Focus | Children identify symmetry in geometric figures using a Mira.

Name: ______________________ Date: ______________________

Symmetry

Circle the pictures that show matching parts.
Use a Mira to help you.

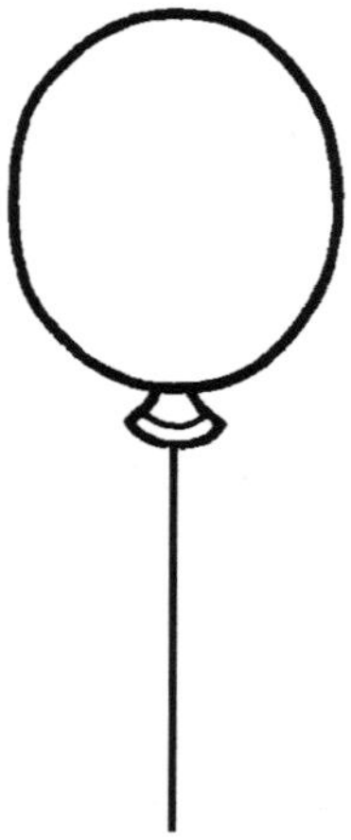

Focus | Children use a Mira to determine which pictures show symmetry.

Name: ______________________ Date: ______________________

Symmetry in Letters

Circle the letters that show symmetry.
Check using a Mira.

O G V C M

P A J B R X

Where would you place a Mira on MOM to show symmetry?
Use 

.

Draw a line where you would put the Mira.

MOM

Think of another word that shows symmetry. ______________________
How can you tell it shows symmetry?

____

Focus Children identify capital letters that show symmetry and use a Mira to check. Then they investigate some words that show symmetry.

HOME CONNECTION
Print your child's name in block letters. With your child, check if the name has symmetry. Look for symmetry in names of other family members.

Name: ______________________ Date: ______________________

Get Moving

Place a cutout on 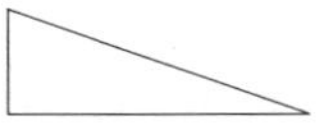.

Move it to cover 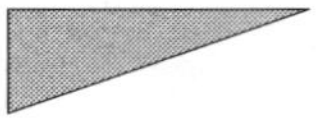.

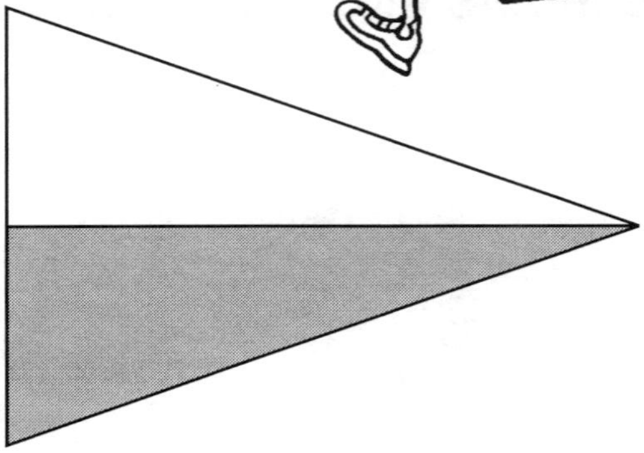

How did the triangle move?

____

Place a cutout on 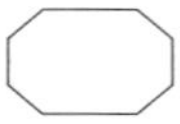.

Move it to cover 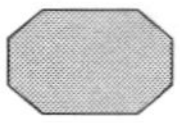.

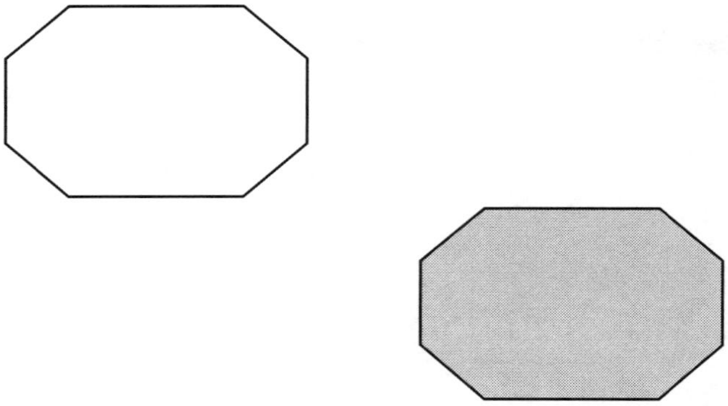

How did the octagon move?

____

Place a cutout on .

Move it to cover .

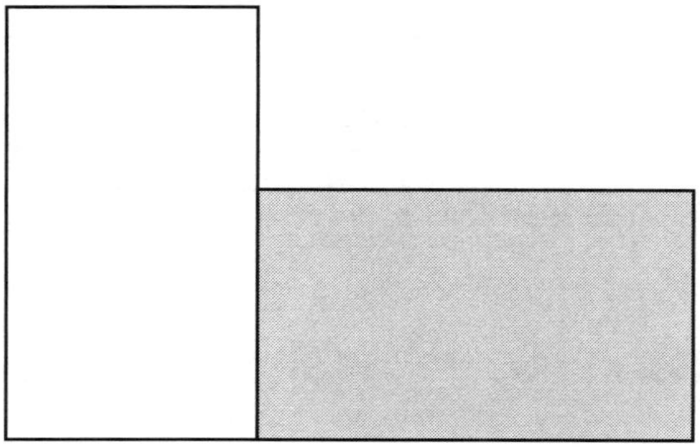

How did the rectangle move?

____

Focus | Children use cutouts from *LM 3: Geometric Figures* to move figures to new positions and describe how they did it.

Name: ______________________________ Date: ______________________________

Move on a 100-Chart

Start at 27.
Show one way to reach 54.

Use 

.

Tell your partner how you did it.

1	2	3	4	5	6	7	8	9	10
11	12	13	14	15	16	17	18	19	20
21	22	23	24	25	26	27	28	29	30
31	32	33	34	35	36	37	38	39	40
41	42	43	44	45	46	47	48	49	50
51	52	53	54	55	56	57	58	59	60
61	62	63	64	65	66	67	68	69	70
71	72	73	74	75	76	77	78	79	80
81	82	83	84	85	86	87	88	89	90
91	92	93	94	95	96	97	98	99	100

Show another way to reach 54.

Use 

.

Tell your partner how you did it.

Focus | Children practise moving from one number to another on a 100-chart. They explain how they moved.

Name: ______________________ Date: ______________________

Find My Number

Choose a number on the 100-chart.
Don't tell!
Print directions to reach your number.

Start at ________.

1. ______________________________
2. ______________________________
3. ______________________________

Ask your partner to find the number.

My partner thinks the number is ________.

Is your partner right? Circle Yes or No.

Try it again with a different number.

Start at ________.

1. ______________________________
2. ______________________________
3. ______________________________

My partner thinks the number is ________.

Is your partner right? Circle Yes or No.

Focus | Children choose numbers on a 100-chart and write directions for others to find them.

Name: ______________________________ Date: ______________________________

Show the Way Home

Help the prairie dog find its way home.

Use 

to show the way.

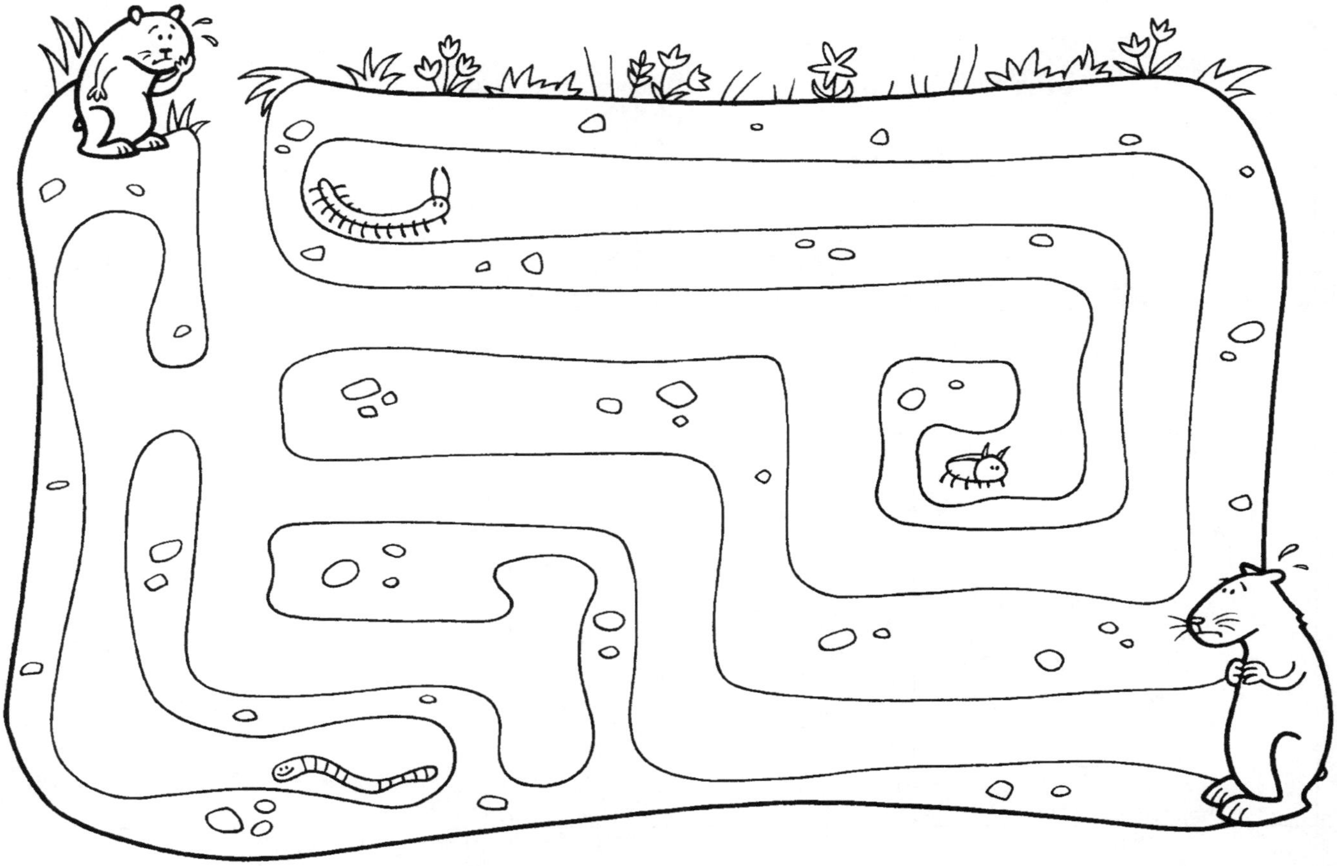

Print your directions for the prairie dog.

____

____

____

FOCUS | Children draw a path and describe a way for the prairie dog to get home through a maze of tunnels.

HOME CONNECTION

Make a map of your home. Hide an object and then show where it is on the map. Ask your child to find it. Take turns hiding and following directions to find objects in your home.

Name: ______________________ Date: ______________________

A Quilt

Follow the directions on page 233 to complete the quilt.

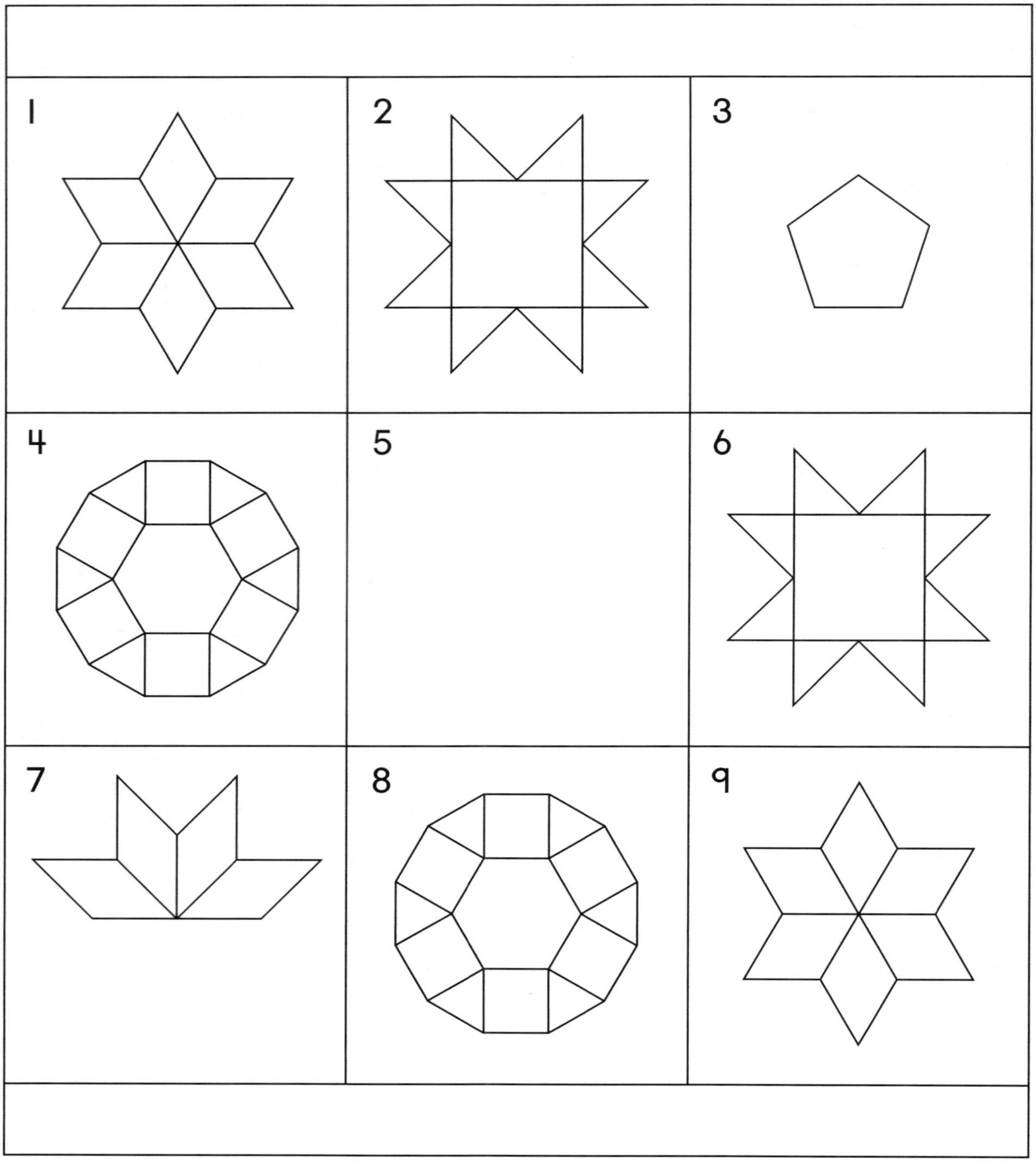

Focus | Children follow directions to complete a quilt.

HOME CONNECTION

With your child, take turns describing each of the quilt blocks on page 232. Ask your child to describe geometric designs in your home.

Name: ______________________________ Date: ______________________________

Finish the Quilt!

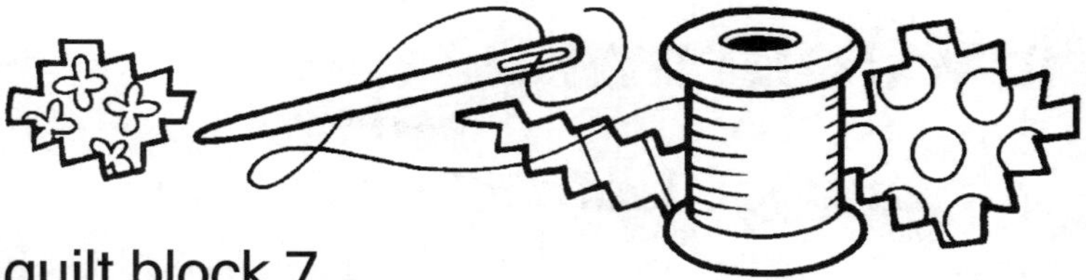

Part 1

Draw the matching part to finish quilt block 7.

Find the quilt block that has only a pentagon.
Draw a triangle on each edge of the pentagon.

What does the design look like? ______________________________

How many vertices are there in this block? ______________________

Use figures to make your own design in the centre quilt block.

Tell what you used. ______________________________

____

____

Part 2

Draw a repeating pattern on the border at the top and bottom of the quilt. Use just one figure. You can make it slide, flip, or turn.

Name two quilt blocks that have the same design.

__________ and __________

Start in Block 1. Go straight down two blocks.
Go one block to the right. Go up one block. Go one block to the left.

What is the number of the block you are in? __________
Name the figures you can find in that block.

____

FOCUS | Children follow directions to complete a quilt and answer related questions.

Name: ______________________ Date: ______________________

My Journal

Tell what you learned about figures.
Use pictures, numbers, or words to show your thinking.

Focus | Children reflect on and record what they learned about 2-D geometric figures.

UNIT 10

Multiplication, Division, and Fractions

Focus | Children use skip counting and other methods to count items in the picture.

Name: ______________________ Date: ______________________

Dear Family,

In this unit, your child will build on number patterns to develop concepts of multiplication, division, and fractions, working with concrete materials.

The Learning Goals for this unit are to

- Learn about multiplication as counting groups of objects.
- Understand that repeated addition, skip counting, and multiplication are the same.
- Learn about division through grouping and sharing.
- Understand the meaning of halves, thirds, and fourths.
- Connect multiplying, dividing, and fractions to daily experiences with making equal groups and sharing.

You can help your child achieve these goals by doing the Home Connection activities suggested at the bottom of selected pages.

Name: ______________________ Date: ______________________

100-Chart Patterns

Shade every second number 

.
What is the skip counting pattern?

Count by ______.

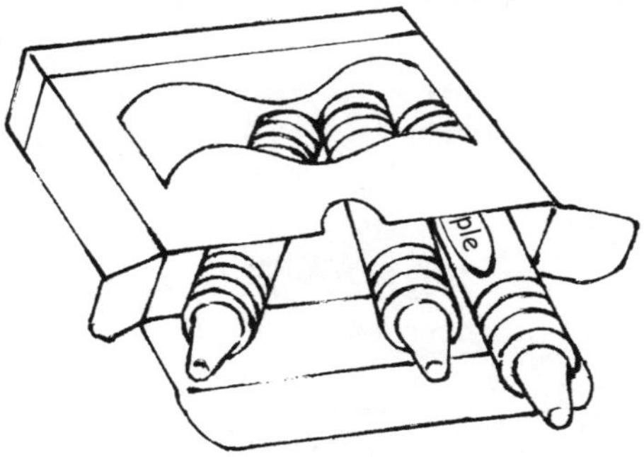

Shade every fifth number 

.
What is the skip counting pattern?

Count by ______.

1	2	3	4	5	6	7	8	9	10
11	12	13	14	15	16	17	18	19	20
21	22	23	24	25	26	27	28	29	30
31	32	33	34	35	36	37	38	39	40
41	42	43	44	45	46	47	48	49	50
51	52	53	54	55	56	57	58	59	60
61	62	63	64	65	66	67	68	69	70
71	72	73	74	75	76	77	78	79	80
81	82	83	84	85	86	87	88	89	90
91	92	93	94	95	96	97	98	99	100

Show another skip counting pattern. What is your pattern?

____

Focus | Children use colour to record skip counting patterns on a 100-chart.

Name: ______________________ Date: ______________________

Button Up

Draw 4 groups of 2 buttons.

Write the addition sentence.

____

4 groups of 2 buttons are

______ buttons altogether.

Draw 3 groups of 4 buttons.

Write the addition sentence.

____

3 groups of 4 buttons are

______ buttons altogether.

Draw 5 groups of 3 buttons.

Write the addition sentence.

____

5 groups of 3 buttons are

______ buttons altogether.

Draw 3 groups of 6 buttons.

Write the addition sentence.

____

3 groups of 6 buttons are

______ buttons altogether.

Focus | Children use repeated addition to count groups of buttons.

HOME CONNECTION

Give your child objects in groups, such as 6 groups of 5 beans. Have your child show you how to find out how many beans in all and to write a repeated addition sentence.

Name: ______________________ Date: ______________________

Make a Problem

How many groups? _____

How many in each group? _____

Think of your problem. Use counters to solve it.

Draw to show how you solved it.

What is the addition sentence for your problem?

____

What is the multiplication sentence for your problem?

____

Focus | Children write and solve a problem using repeated addition and multiplication.

Name: ______________________ Date: ______________________

Multiply It!

How many items are in each box?

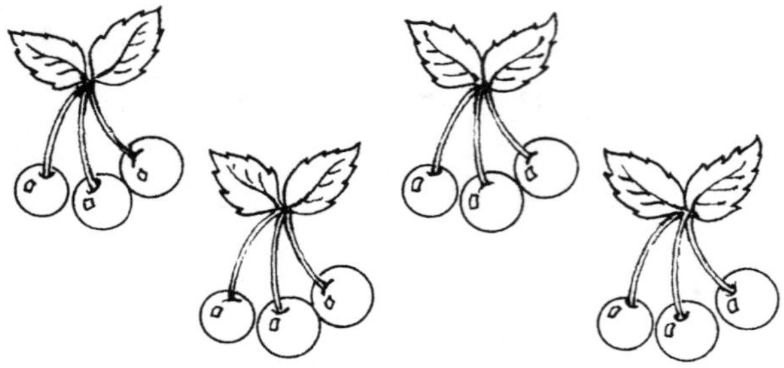

Write the addition sentence.

____

Write a multiplication sentence.

____

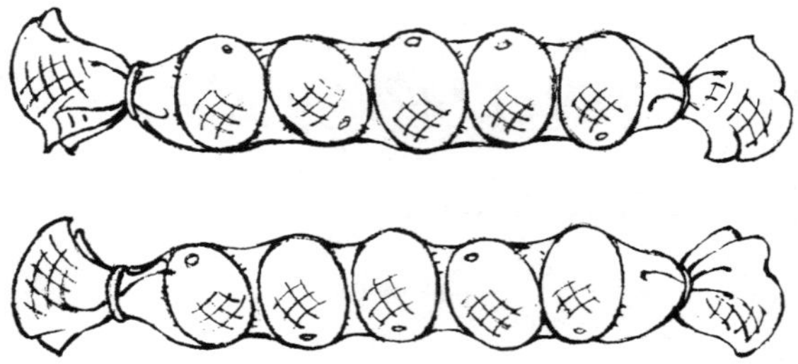

Write the addition sentence.

____

Write a multiplication sentence.

____

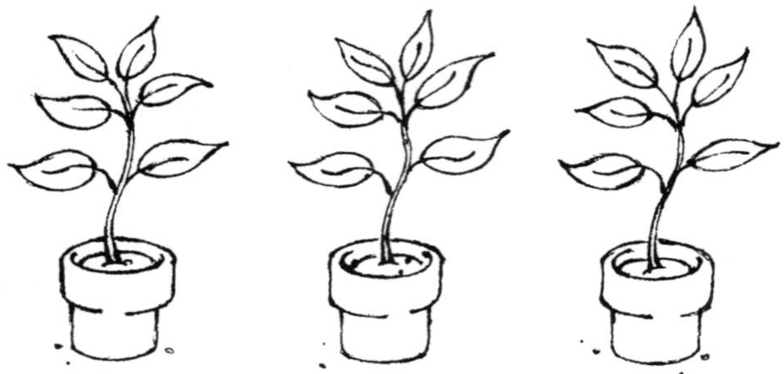

Write the addition sentence.

____

Write a multiplication sentence.

____

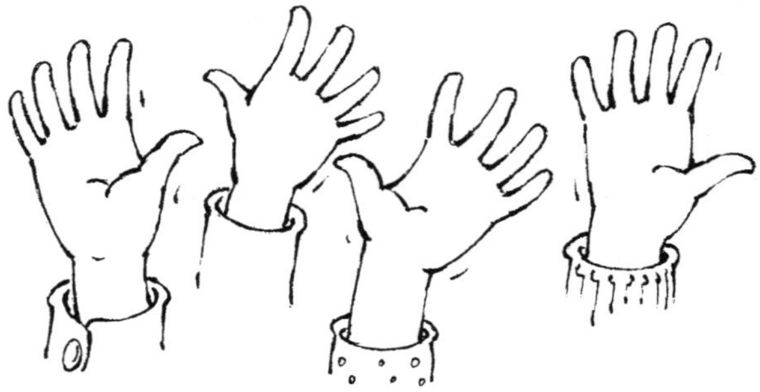

Write the addition sentence.

____

Write a multiplication sentence.

____

Focus | Children write about multiplication problems in two ways.

HOME CONNECTION

Find examples of items that come packaged in groups, such as stamps. Ask your child to write a repeated addition sentence and a multiplication sentence to find how many items there are altogether.

Name: ______________________________ Date: ______________________________

Share the Toys

How many toys are there altogether? _____

How many do you think each person will get? _____

Show how you divided the toys.

How many did each person get? _____

Write a sentence to show how the toys are shared.

____

Focus | Children use materials to model how they can divide toys into 4 equal groups to share them.

Name: ______________________ Date: ______________________

Share and Share Alike

Four children each want an equal share of apples to take home. How many apples should each child get?

Write a sentence about your answer. ______________________

____

Six children want to share these crayons fairly. How many crayons should each child get?

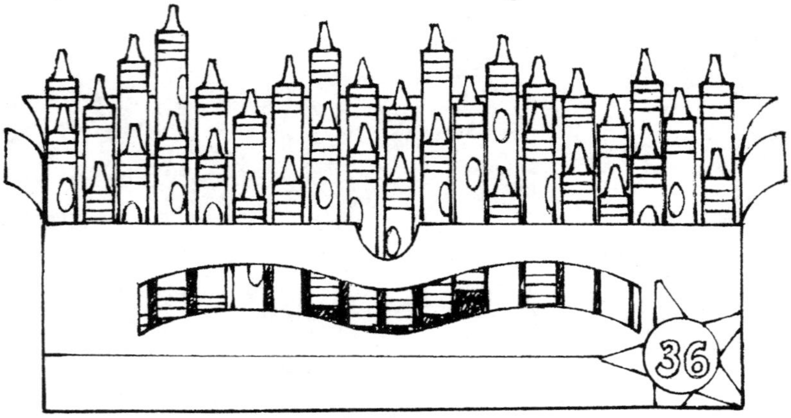

Write a sentence about your answer. ______________________

____

Focus | Children practise dividing items into equal groups (sharing) and recording the result.

HOME CONNECTION

Have your child find out how many pieces of fruit, such as grapes, can be fairly divided among a group of friends or family.

Name: ______________________ Date: ______________________

How Many Bunches?

You are making bunches of flowers.
You have 36 flowers.

You put 6 flowers in every bunch.
How many bunches can you make?
Write a sentence about your answer.

____

Suppose you put 4 flowers in every bunch.
How many bunches can you make?
Write a sentence about your answer.

____

Focus | Children divide 36 flowers into groups of 6 and of 4.

HOME CONNECTION

Have your child sort a number of objects (divisible by 4) into groups of 4. Ask your child how many groups he or she made.

Name: ______________________ Date: ______________________

Parts of a Whole

Write if each figure is in halves, thirds, or fourths.

This is in __________. There are _____ equal parts.

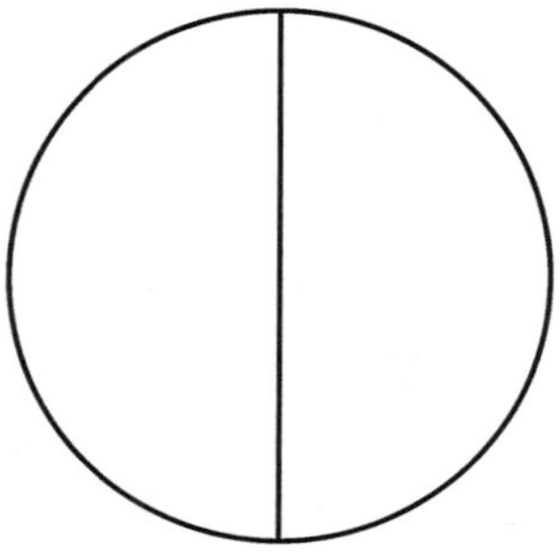

This is in __________. There are _____ equal parts.

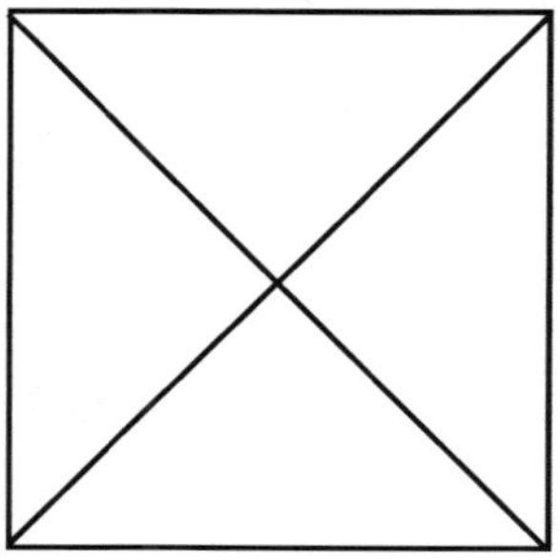

This is in __________. There are _____ equal parts.

HOME CONNECTION

Let your child work with fractions during meals. Show your child a sandwich in halves, a pear cut into fourths, and so on. Have him or her name the fraction.

Focus | Children describe fractional parts.

Name: ______________________ Date: ______________________

Colouring Fractions

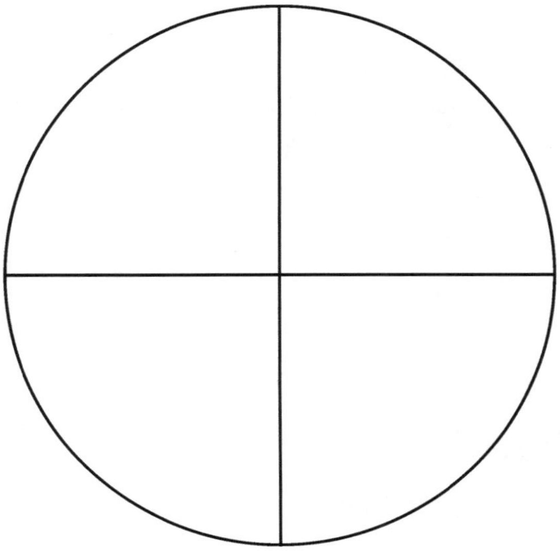

Colour one-fourth.

Colour one-half.

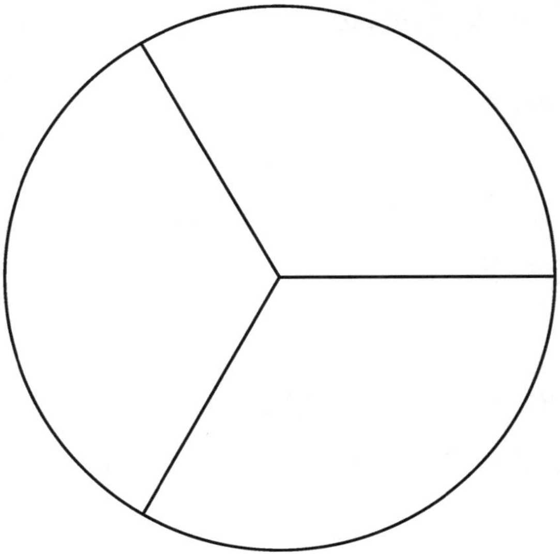

Colour two-thirds.

Colour three-fourths.

Focus | Children colour fractional parts of a whole.

Name: ______________________ Date: ______________________

Tiny Toys

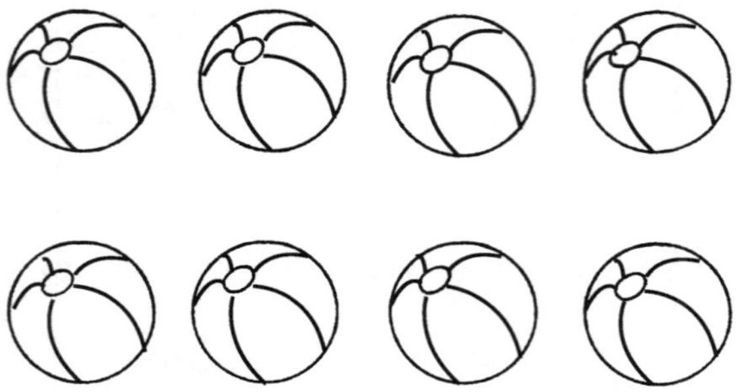

Show 2 equal groups.
How many balls in each half?

____

Show 3 equal groups.
How many dolls in each third?

____

Show 2 equal groups.
How many ducks in each half?

____

Show 4 equal groups.
How many cars in each fourth?

____

HOME CONNECTION

Find examples of items that come packaged in groups, such as rolls. Ask your child to tell you how many are in one-half of the package.

Focus | Children determine fractions of a set.

Name: ______________________________ Date: ______________________________

Bumper Cars

There are 13 children lined up for the bumper cars.
There are 4 bumper cars.
Each bumper car can hold 3 children.
Can everyone ride bumper cars at the same time?

Show how you solved the problem.
Use pictures, numbers, or words.

Focus | Children use the strategy "act it out" to solve a problem, and record their work.

Name: ______________________ Date: ______________________

Getting on a Plane

Altogether, 22 people need to fly on this plane.
There are 6 rows of seats. There are 4 seats in each row.
Can everyone get on the plane?

Show your thinking in pictures, numbers, or words.

Focus | Children solve a problem involving division concepts.

HOME CONNECTION

Invite your child to tell you how he or she solved the problem on this page and to make up a similar problem for you to solve. Use pennies to stand for the people who want to get on the plane.

Name: ______________________ Date: ______________________

Musical Ride Problems

Look at the picture.

Tell a number story about equal groups. Show your story and how you solved it.

How many groups? _____ How many in each group? _____

How many altogether? _____

Write a number sentence about your story. ______________

Focus | Children create and solve a story about equal groups.

HOME CONNECTION

Have your child tell you the story he or she created and how to solve it. Ask: "Is there another way you could write this story?"

Name: ______________________ Date: ______________________

Equal Groups of Horses

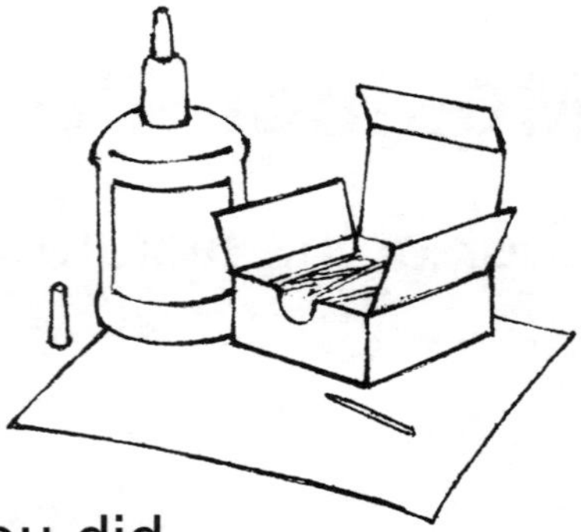

You need to put 24 horses in equal groups.
Use toothpicks to show equal groups.
Glue the toothpicks on a piece of paper.

Use pictures, numbers, or words to show what you did.

Focus | Children divide 24 into equal groups.

Name: ______________________________ Date: ______________________________

After the Ride

There are 24 horses.
One-third of the horses get new saddles.
Use counters to find the answer.

How many horses get new saddles?

There are 24 horses.
Four horses go in each trailer to travel home from the show.
Use counters to find the answer.

How many trailers do the horses need?

Four horses will eat equal shares of hay.
Fold a piece of paper to show how to divide the hay.

What fraction of the hay will each horse get? _____

Focus | Children solve division and fraction problems.

Name: ______________________________ Date: ______________________________

My Journal

Tell what you learned about multiplying and dividing.
Use pictures, numbers, or words.

Tell what you learned about fractions.
Use pictures, numbers, or words.

Focus | Children reflect on and record what they learned about multiplication, division, and fractions.

UNIT 11

Mass and Capacity

Focus | Children look for ways people are measuring and comparing items in the store, and identify measurable attributes.

Name: ______________________________ Date: ______________________________

Dear Family,

In this unit, your child will be learning more about measurement. Your child will develop an understanding of *capacity*, how much a container can hold, and *mass*, which relates to the heaviness of an object.

The Learning Goals for this unit are to

- Estimate, compare, measure, and order the capacities of containers by filling them with materials to see how much they hold.
- Estimate, compare, measure, and order the masses of objects using simple scales with non-standard units.
- Solve everyday problems about mass and capacity.

You can help your child achieve these goals by doing the Home Connection activities suggested at the bottom of selected pages.

Name: ______________________ Date: ______________________

What You Measure

Show things you measure.
Use pictures, numbers, or words.

Capacity

Home	School

Mass

Home	School

Focus | Children brainstorm times at home and at school when the capacity and mass of items are measured. Then they record the items that are measured.

Name: ______________________ Date: ______________________

Comparing Capacity

Predict which container will hold the most.

____

Predict which container will hold the least.

____

Draw or write the name of each container.
Measure and record how many scoops fill each one.

Container A	Container B	Container C	Container D
______	______	______	______

Which container holds the most?

____

Which container holds the least?

____

List the containers in order from the greatest capacity to the least capacity.

__________ __________ __________ __________

Focus | Children measure and compare the capacities of four containers.

Name: ______________________ Date: ______________________

Measure and Graph

In the chart, draw or write the name of each container.
Measure how many scoops fill each one.
Tally and record the number of scoops.

Container	Tally	Number of

Graph how many scoops fill each container.

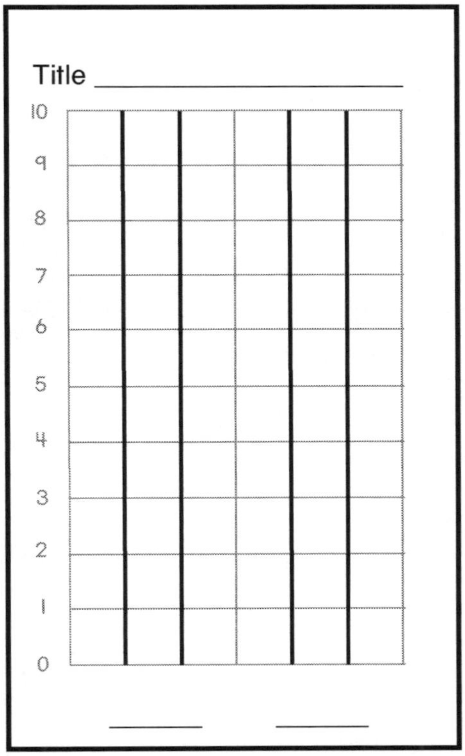

What does the graph tell you?

____

Focus | Children measure the capacities of two containers and graph the results to compare the capacities.

HOME CONNECTION

Gather some kitchen containers. Have your child compare two or more at a time, working over the sink, to see which holds more by pouring water from one into another.

Name: ______________________ Date: ______________________

About How Many Scoops?

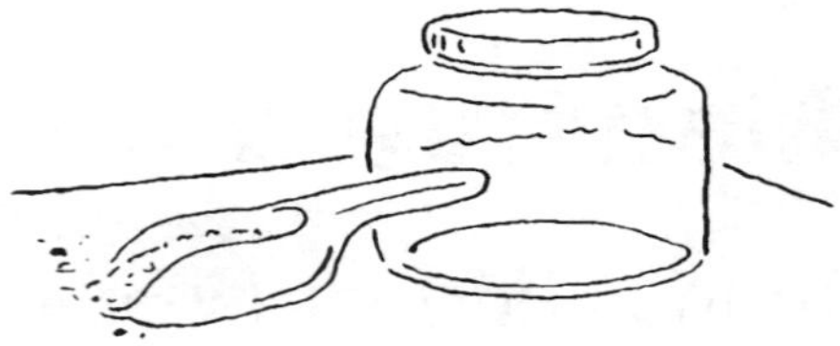

My scoop looks like ____________________.

I estimate my container will hold about _______ scoops.

Fill your container half full. How many scoops do you need? _______

Change your estimate if you want. ____________________

Fill your container full. How many scoops does it hold? __________

Check with another group.

Their scoop looks like ____________________.

They needed _______ scoops.

What did you find out about estimating capacity?
Use pictures, numbers, or words.

Focus | Children estimate and check the number of scoops of material needed to fill a container. They compare their results with those of another group.

Name: ____________________ Date: ____________________

Ordering Capacity

In the chart, draw or write the name of each container.
Predict which one will hold the least.

____.

Predict which one will hold the most.

____.

Measure the capacity of each container.
Tally and record the number of scoops.

Container	Tally 	Number of 

List the containers in order from least capacity to greatest capacity.

______________ ______________ ______________

HOME CONNECTION

Enlist your child's help in everyday routines, such as making juice. Ask: "How many containers of water do we add? Is our pitcher big enough? Will it be full to the top when we are done?"

Focus | Children estimate the capacities of containers and measure the capacities using a scoop. Then they order the containers from least to greatest capacity.

Name: ______________________ Date: ______________________

Fair Shares to Drink

Estimate how many units of water will go in each glass. __________

Draw the glasses you are using to act out the problem.

____ units	____ units	____ units	____ units	____ units

Share the water among all 5 glasses.
Record the level of water in each glass.
Record the number of units in each glass.

Explain how you solved the problem.
Use pictures, numbers, or words.

Focus | Children work with materials to share a given amount of water equally among 5 glasses and show the level for each glass when filled by an equal measure. Then they explain how they solved the problem.

Name: ______________________ Date: ______________________

Fair Shares to Snack

How many units do you think each bowl will get? __________

Draw the bowls you are using to act out the problem.

____ units	____ units	____ units	____ units	____ units

Share the popcorn among all 5 bowls.
Record the level in each bowl.
Record the number of units in each bowl.

Explain how you solved the problem.
Use pictures, numbers, or words.

Focus | Children share a given amount of popcorn equally among 5 bowls. Then they explain how they solved the problem.

HOME CONNECTION
With your child, divide treats equally among several containers. Have your child show the level for each container when filled by an equal measure.

Name: ______________________ Date: ______________________

Comparing Mass

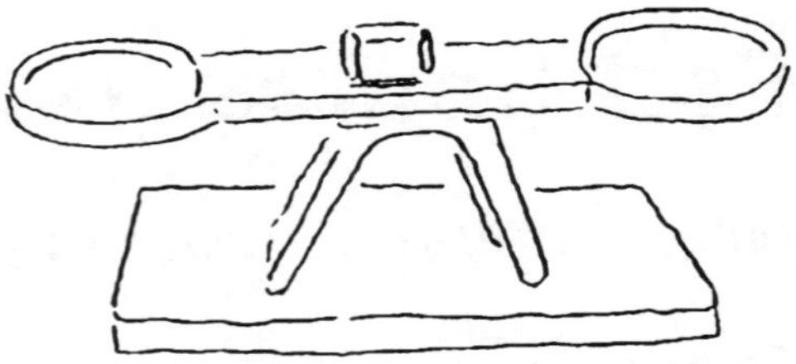

Predict which object will be the lightest.
Predict which object will be the heaviest.

Use your predictions to order the objects from lightest to heaviest.
Draw or write the name of each object in order.

the lightest object			the heaviest object

Use a balance scale to compare the objects.
Line up the objects on your desk from lightest to heaviest.
List the objects in order from lightest to heaviest.

__________ __________ __________ __________

How did the balance scale help you? Use pictures, numbers, or words.

Focus | Children order the masses of items using their hands. They repeat the activity using a balance scale.

Name: ______________________ Date: ______________________

Classroom Objects

Choose 4 objects from around you.
Predict which object will be the lightest and which will be the heaviest.

Draw or write the name of each object.

the lightest object			the heaviest object

Use a balance scale to compare the objects.
List the objects in order from lightest to heaviest.

__________ __________ __________ __________

Now find another object to compare.
Do you think it is the heaviest, the lightest, or near the middle?

____

Check with a balance scale.
List the 5 objects in order from greatest to least mass.

__________ __________ __________ __________ __________

Focus | Children order the masses of classroom items using a balance scale.

HOME CONNECTION

Have your child find objects lighter than, the same as, or heavier than an object. Check with a simple hanger scale. (Tie a plastic bag to each end of a hanger and balance the hanger on your finger.)

Name: ______________________ Date: ______________________

Balancing Act

Draw or write the name of each object you are measuring.
Estimate the mass of each object.
Write each estimate in the chart.

Object	Estimated Mass	Measure
the lightest object		
the heaviest object		

Measure the mass of each object. Write each measure in the chart.

Focus | Children compare and measure the masses of several classroom objects.

Name: ______________________ Date: ______________________

About How Many?

Estimate the masses of 2 objects.
Use 3 different units.

	Object 1	Object 2
Unit 1 estimate		
Unit 2 estimate		
Unit 3 estimate		

Use a balance scale.

Find the masses of the 2 objects.
Use the 3 different units.

	Object 1	Object 2
Unit 1 measure		
Unit 2 measure		
Unit 3 measure		

Compare with a friend.

Were your answers different?
Why do you think that happened?

____

HOME CONNECTION

Have your child estimate masses at home. For example, ask: "About how many lemons are as heavy as a grapefruit? About how many grapes are as heavy as an orange?"

Focus | Children estimate and measure masses using 3 different non-standard units.

Name: ______________________ Date: ______________________

Plant-Pot Parade

Estimate to order the pots from least to greatest capacity.

_______ _______ _______ _______ _______

Draw or write the name of each plant pot in order.

Measure the capacity of each container.
Record the capacity beside its name or picture.

Which container holds the most?
How do you know?

____

____

FOCUS | Children estimate the capacities of containers and explain how to solve a capacity problem.

Name: ______________________ Date: ______________________

Which Is the Heaviest?

Estimate to order the objects from lightest to heaviest.

______ ______ ______ ______ ______

Draw or write the name of each object in order.

Measure the mass of each object.
Record the mass beside its name or picture.

Which object is the heaviest?
How do you know?

____

____

Focus | Children estimate and measure the masses of 5 objects to find the heaviest.

Name: ____________________ Date: ____________________

My Journal

Tell what you learned about comparing how much different containers can hold.

Use pictures, numbers, or words to show your thinking.

Tell what you learned about comparing how heavy objects are.

Use pictures, numbers, or words to show your thinking.

Focus | Children reflect on and record what they learned about capacity and mass.

HOME CONNECTION

Invite your child to practise measuring capacity and mass while helping with grocery shopping or preparing simple recipes.

The Field Trip

The Grade 2 class was so excited.
Even Grandma was invited.
Field Trip Day was finally here.
Everyone would visit Aquarium Place this year.

Take-Home Story

Inside they hardly made a sound.
There were glass and water tanks all around.
And so many different fish were there.
All colours and sizes—they were everywhere!

A whale swam by and looked their way.
“Welcome,” its expression seemed to say.
Over in the corner they saw a crowd.
“A shark!” they suddenly gasped out loud.

Then some scuba divers came
and swam with fish that seemed quite tame.
"That looks like Grandma!" said Cam's friend Ben.
Cam blinked his eyes and looked again.

"I wonder," said Cam as he stopped to stare.
"Just how many fish might fit in there?
How many tubs of water, too?"
"I'll bet there are more than one thousand!" cried Lu.

Soon it was time for the dolphins to eat.
Buckets of fish were the lunchtime treat.
Some helpers held fish out over the tanks,
and dolphins jumped up and chirped out, "Thanks!"

What an amazing day it had been.
There were all kinds of undersea life they had seen.
They lined up again to get back on the bus, as they wondered, "What did the fish think when they looked at *us*!"

About the Story

The story was read in class to prepare for a Mathematics Investigation activity. Children used positional language, solved number and measurement problems, and made a model using 3-D solids.

Talk about It Together

- What is your favourite part of the story?
- What is Grandma doing while the children look at all the fish in the tanks?
- Do you think working at Aquarium Place would be interesting? Why? Why not?
- What kind of jobs would the aquarium workers do?

At the Library

Ask your local librarian about other good books to share about measuring objects, mass and capacity, geometric solids, and numbers.

Where Will You Be?

Put X's on the map on 3 things you want to see.
Draw a line showing how to get from one to another.
Write a note telling where you will be.

Dear Teacher,
First, I will visit ______________________
Follow these directions to find me.

____

____

Second, I will visit ____________________________.
Follow these directions to find me.

____

____

Third, I will visit ______________________________.
Follow these directions to find me.

____

____

How Big Is a Whale?

Fun Facts about Orca Whales

An orca whale can be 7 m long.
An orca whale can be 2 m wide.
An orca whale can eat 18 buckets of fish every day.
An orca whale can have the same mass as 150 Grade 2 children!

Look at the fun facts about orca whales.
About how many children could lie in a row beside one whale? Show your thinking.

Estimate how many whales could fit in your classroom.
Use pictures, numbers, or words to show how you could check your estimate.

Create a whale measurement problem of your own and solve it.

Moving to a New Home

There are 48 fish in the tank.

Place the fish equally into 3 new tanks.

How many will be in each tank? ______________
Use counters to help you solve the problem.
Show your thinking in pictures, numbers, or words.

Place the fish equally into 8 new tanks.

How many will be in each tank? ______________
Use counters to help you solve the problem.
Show your thinking in pictures, numbers, or words.

Building the Aquarium

Here is the outside of an aquarium.

Use 3-D solids to make a model of an aquarium building.
What solids did you use?

____

____

Use pictures, numbers, or words to tell how you made your model.

Symmetrical Art

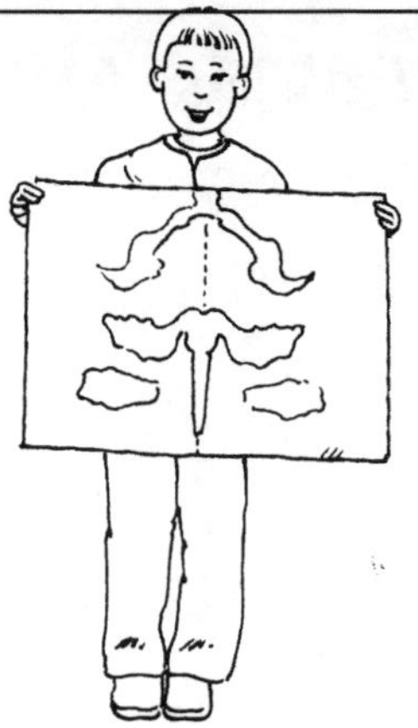

Fold a piece of paper in half.
Then open it and put a few
dabs of paint on one half.
Fold the paper again and
press the halves together.

Open it and you will see a
symmetrical masterpiece!

Want to make it more interesting?
Cut out some figures and glue them on your artwork.
Remember, whenever you put something on one side,
it must have a symmetrical match on the other side!

Eggs for All

Take an empty egg carton
and put a counter
in each space.
Let's imagine brunch
is at your place.
Each guest eats the same
number of eggs, and all
the eggs are used.

If each person eats 2 eggs,
how many people were at the brunch?

What if each person eats
3 eggs? 4 eggs? 6 eggs?

Use the counters to help
you divide.

Fold

Math at Home

Math at Home 3

No Fair

Wendy's little brother
thought she had more
juice than he did.
She tried to tell him
that she really had less.
What do you think
she said to him?

Sandwich Fractions

Get creative with your lunch.
Cut your sandwich a different way each day.
You might try

The sky's the limit!

Tell Me About This Figure Game Board

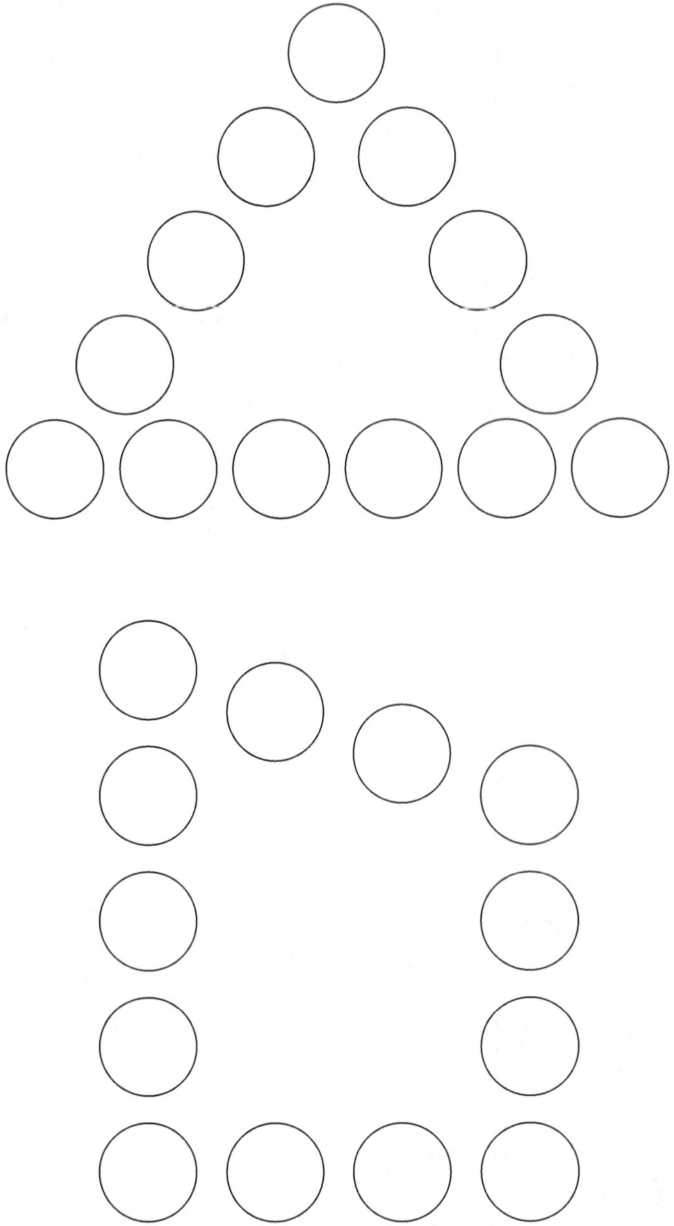

Tell Me About This Figure

Game

You'll need:
- 2-D figures in a bag you cannot see through

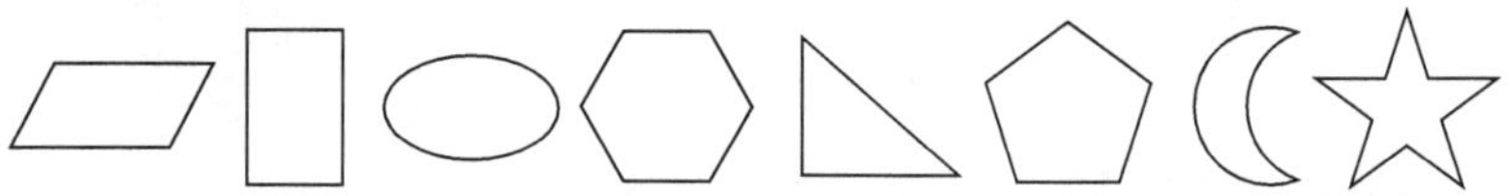

- small counters
- game board (page 7)

Before the game begins, each player chooses an outlined figure on the game board (page 7).

On your turn:
- Pull a figure out from the bag and lay it between you and your partner.
- Both of you secretly write one thing that you notice about the figure. (Think about number of sides, lengths of the sides, number of corners.)

- Read your descriptions to each other.
  If they are **different**,
  you place two counters on your outlined figure.
  If they are the **same**, the other player places one counter on his or her outlined figure.

Take turns until someone's outlined figure is full.

Moving Day

Ryan could move this box:

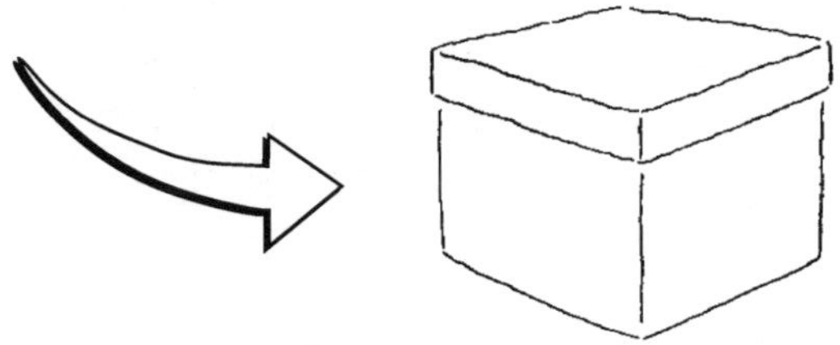

But he could not move this one:

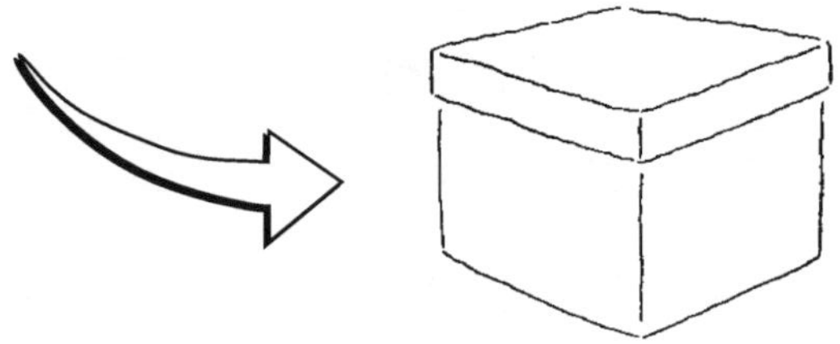

What do you think is in each box?

Stick Figures

Suppose it takes 3 craft sticks to make one side of a square.

How many craft sticks will it take to make the whole square?

Suppose it takes 3 craft sticks to make one side of a hexagon. How many craft sticks might it take to make the whole hexagon?

What other ways are there to make the whole hexagon?

Transformation Moves

Challenge a friend to follow your directions.

You might say: Turn to the left.
Slide to the right.
Turn to the right.
Slide forward.

Get creative! Switch roles and see how much fun directions can be.

How Long Is It?

Find something in your house that is about

- 3 footprints long
- 4 fingers wide
- 2 arms long
- 5 hands wide

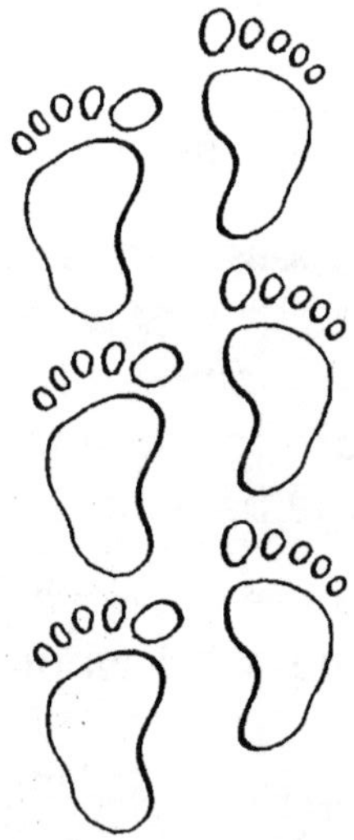

Guess first, then measure the object.

What do you think would happen if a grown-up looked for something 4 footprints long?

Amazing Area

This painting is made completely of squares.

It has an area of ______ squares.

Imagine the artist wants a frame.
The distance all the way around is _____ units.
(Count each side of a square as one unit.)

Let's imagine the artist makes another painting using the same squares.

What happens to the area of the painting?

What about the distance around?

How Much Is 100 Drops?

Imagine putting 100 drops of water in a drinking glass.
How full will it be?

Take a guess, then try it!
Were you surprised?